The
Essential
Book of
Presidential
Trivia

★ ★ ★

The Essential Book of Presidential Trivia

★ ★ ★

Noah McCullough

★ ★ ★

Random House Trade Paperbacks

New York

A Random House Trade Paperback Original

Copyright © 2006 by Noah McCullough

Published in the United States by Random House Trade Paperbacks,
an imprint of The Random House Publishing Group,
a division of Random House, Inc., New York.

RANDOM HOUSE TRADE PAPERBACKS and colophon are trademarks of
Random House, Inc.

Caricatures of U.S. presidents by Ron Coddington, distributed by TMS
(Tribune Media Services). Reprinted by permission of Tribune Media Services.

LIBRARY OF CONGRESS CATALOGING-IN-PUBLICATION DATA

McCullough, Noah.
The essential book of presidential trivia / Noah McCullough.
p. cm.
ISBN 1-4000-6482-1 (pbk.)
1. Presidents—United States—Miscellanea. I. Title.

E176.1.M423 2006
973.09'9—dc22
[B]   2005052911

Printed in the United States of America

www.atrandom.com

6 8 9 7

Book design by Mary A. Wirth

To my little brother, Nicholas,
my best friend, who waited patiently
to play with me while I was writing this book.
Now we can play, buddy! I love you!

The Essential Book of Presidential Trivia

BIRTHDAY: February 22, 1732
(Gregorian calendar),
in Westmoreland County, Virginia

PARENTS: Augustine and Mary Ball Washington

FIRST LADY: Martha Dandridge Custis

KIDS: None of his own, but adopted Martha's:
John and Martha Custis

COLLEGE: None

JOBS BEFORE PRESIDENT: Surveyor, Farmer,
Soldier, Member of House of Burgesses,
Continental Congressman

POLITICAL PARTY: Federalist

RELIGION: Episcopalian

AGE AT INAUGURATION: Fifty-seven

YEARS IN OFFICE: 1789–1797

NICKNAME: Father of His Country

DIED: December 14, 1799

George Washington

#1

—was America's first true *action hero*. Admired by his fellow men, he was brave, commanding, and daring. Washington is considered a legend in his own time, not for chopping down a cherry tree or having wooden teeth, but for sculpting a government that is still in use today. (The cherry tree and wooden teeth are urban myths.) Although he was a rugged war hero, Washington was perhaps the first "Renaissance man" to be president. He was an avid art collector and a fabulous dancer (it is said that ladies waited in long lines to dance with the president at public functions). Washington also had a flair for fashion and designed many military uniforms, as well as decorating his Mount Vernon estate himself.

A little-known fact about George is that he actually selected and surveyed the place for our nation's capital (the White House, too). He will be remembered not only for forming the best cabinet in history but also for defining the highest office in the land, the presidency of the United States of America.

By the time George was fifty-seven he had lost nearly all of his teeth. This was most likely due to his habit of cracking walnuts with them as well as not taking good care of them. This is interesting because George hired staff to brush his horses' teeth daily. Embarrassed about having few teeth, Washington was on a quest to find a comfortable set of false teeth. Some were made of lead, some of ivory; some were animal and human teeth. None were made of wood as the legend has led us to believe. When he was inaugurated, he still had one tooth of his own, and his French dentist made him an ivory set to fit around that natural tooth.

Did You Know That . . .

★ Washington banned curse words from the army (although he said a *lot* of the words he banned)?

★ George Washington was the only president to win 100 percent of the electoral college for both of his elections?

★ George Washington was eleven when his dad died?

★ Washington's mom was unpredictable and nagged and bothered him into his presidency?

★ First Lady Martha Washington was five feet tall?

★ Martha Washington missed her husband's inauguration because she could not get to New York in time?

★ First Lady Martha Washington's first husband, Daniel Custis, died, leaving her a widow with two children?

★ Washington suffered smallpox and lived through it?

★ Washington once had a relationship with Sally Fairfax?

★ Washington's annual salary was approximately $25,000 (about $1,000,000 in today's economy)?

★ Washington spent 7 percent of that annual salary on alcohol?

★ Washington had fine furs put on all his horses?

★ President Jimmy Carter bestowed on Washington the rank of "six-star general" and "General of the Armies of Congress"? (He felt that our first president should be the highest-ranking military official of all time.)

★ Washington loved to hunt foxes?

★ As president, Washington had the United States remain neutral during the English and French quarrels?

★ President Washington would not shake hands because he thought this beneath the president? (He preferred bowing.)

★ George Washington traveled throughout his presidency and visited each state in the Union during that time?

★ Washington collected paintings on these travels? (They can be seen at Mount Vernon.)

★ President Washington's favorite horse was a white horse named Nelson?

★ George Washington added the words "so help me God" to the presidential oath of office?

★ Washington decided that the president should be called "the president," not "the king" or "His Majesty"?

★ George Washington was the largest distiller of alcohol in the state of Virginia? (He produced over 11,000 gallons of whiskey at Mount Vernon.)

★ Washington actually borrowed money to get to his own inauguration?

★ President Washington's first inauguration speech was only ninety seconds long and consisted of 183 words?

★ George Washington ran a ferry service across the Potomac River during his first year in office?

★ America actually had a vice president before it had its first president? (George Washington was sworn in as the first president of the United States on April 30, 1789—nine days after John Adams had been sworn in as vice president, on April 21, 1789.)

★ Washington's second inauguration speech was even shorter than his first—135 words, down from the 183 of his first inaugural speech?

★ George Washington had two horses shot from under him and four bullets pass through his uniform as he was fighting in the French and Indian War of 1754?

★ Washington wore a size-13 shoe?

★ Washington didn't take a bath often because he believed that it was unhealthy for him?

★ Washington had an eighth-grade education?

★ George Washington was a young millionaire because of marrying the rich widow Martha Custis?

★ President Washington never lived in the White House?

★ Washington wore a suit that was "made in America" for his inauguration?

★ Washington died of tonsillitis and pneumonia at the age of sixty-seven?

★ Washington was the only president to have a state named after him?

★ The population of the United States when Washington was in office was almost 4 million?

★ George Washington was the first president to appear on a postage stamp? (Ten-cent stamp, U.S. Post Office, 1847.)

★ Washington was one of two presidents to sign the U.S. Constitution? (Washington, Madison.)

★ Washington had 300 slaves when he died?

★ Washington was very nervous at his inauguration and mumbled through his oath of office?

★ The famous portrait of George Washington was started a year before his death but was finished after his death? (John Adams's son-in-law posed for the unfinished body and limbs.)

★ Washington's eyes were a gray-blue color?

BIRTHDAY: October 30, 1735,
in Braintree (now Quincy), Massachusetts

PARENTS: John and Susanna Boylston Adams

FIRST LADY: Abigail Smith

KIDS: Abigail Amelia, John Quincy, Susanna,
Charles, and Thomas Boylston Adams

COLLEGE: Harvard

JOBS BEFORE PRESIDENT: Farmer, Teacher, Lawyer,
Member of Massachusetts House of Representatives,
Continental Congressman, Minister to France,
the Netherlands, and England,
Vice President under George Washington

POLITICAL PARTY: Federalist

RELIGION: Unitarian

AGE AT INAUGURATION: Sixty-one

YEARS IN OFFICE: 1797–1801

NICKNAMES: His Rotundity; Father of the Navy

DIED: July 4, 1826

John Adams

#2

—was sort of defeated before he even started. Stepping into the size 13 shoes that George Washington left was an impossible task, or at least it must have seemed like it. How would you like to follow a popular war hero known as the Father of His Country? For his whole life Adams personally felt like a failure. He was moody, had poor people skills, and spoke with a lisp because he had few of his own teeth.

One very strong character trait that stood out in Adams was courage. He stood against members of his own party and other politicians of the time who thought he should go to war with France. If he had not shown courage and negotiated peace with France, our history and our menus would be totally different from what they are today.

The press, many politicians of the day, and even members of his own party were very critical of his decisions. This infuriated President Adams. He became so paranoid that in 1798 Adams signed the Alien and Sedition Acts, which made it a crime to write against or falsely speak against federal officeholders, including the president. This made Adams very unpopular. How would you like it if you couldn't say anything bad about our leaders? (What would the evening news do?) Even his own vice president, Thomas Jefferson, angrily argued that these acts were unconstitutional and violated the First Amendment right to free speech. C'mon, Mr. President!

Adams's luck didn't change. Even though he was the first president to live in the new White House, four months after moving in he lost his bid for reelection to his vice president, Thomas Jefferson. Adams was so bitter after losing the election that he left the White House in the middle of the night before Jefferson's inauguration so he wouldn't have to see him.

Did You Know That . . .

★ President Adams was chubby and was referred to by opponents as His Rotundity?

★ John Adams was a lawyer for British soldiers involved in the Boston Massacre?

★ Adams's last words were "Jefferson still survives"? (Jefferson had died a few hours earlier.)

★ Adams earned two degrees from Harvard?

★ There were only six operable rooms in the White House when John Adams moved in?

★ Adams was fluent in seven languages?

★ Adams often played with his grandchildren in the White House? (He sometimes took a kitchen chair, put them on it, and pretended to be their horse, pulling it.)

★ Adams was one of four presidents to live ninety years or more? (The others were Reagan, Ford, and Hoover.)

★ Adams was the first president who did not win reelection?

★ John Adams was the first president to have a son elected president?

★ Adams was America's very first vice president? (He served two terms.)

★ Adams was considered the Father of the Navy? (It was created when he was vice president.)

★ President Adams had a favorite horse named Cleopatra? (He had stables built at the White House just for her.)

★ First Lady Abigail Adams spoke out in favor of women's rights?

★ Abigail Adams dried her laundry in the White House East Room?

★ John Adams died the exact same day as Thomas Jefferson— July 4, 1826? (This day was the fiftieth anniversary of the signing of the Declaration of Independence.)

★ President Adams began smoking when he was eight years old?

★ Adams was one of two presidents (he and his son) born on the very same street in the very same city? (Franklin Street in Quincy [formerly Braintree], Massachusetts.)

★ It was John Adams's idea to celebrate the Fourth of July with
   fireworks, games, sports, and picnics?

★ John Adams was five feet six inches tall?

★ President Adams had blue eyes?

★ John Adams wrote in his journal on his second night in the
   White House (November 2, 1800), "I pray Heaven to bestow
   the best Blessings on this House and all that shall hereafter
   inhabit it. May none but honest and wise men ever rule
   beneath this roof"? (FDR had this message carved into
   the mantel in the White House State Dining Room.)

★ ★ ★ ★ ★ ★ ★ ★ ★ ★ ★ ★ ★ ★ ★

Presidents Who Were Governors First

THOMAS JEFFERSON: Virginia

JAMES MONROE: Virginia

MARTIN VAN BUREN: New York

WILLIAM HENRY HARRISON: Indiana Territory

JOHN TYLER: Virginia

JAMES POLK: Tennessee

ANDREW JOHNSON: Tennessee

RUTHERFORD B. HAYES: Ohio

GROVER CLEVELAND: New York

WILLIAM MCKINLEY: Ohio

THEODORE ROOSEVELT: New York

WILLIAM TAFT: Philippines

WOODROW WILSON: New Jersey

CALVIN COOLIDGE: Massachusetts

FRANKLIN D. ROOSEVELT: New York

JIMMY CARTER: Georgia

RONALD REAGAN: California

BILL CLINTON: Arkansas

GEORGE W. BUSH: Texas

BIRTHDAY: April 13, 1743, in Goochland
(now Albemarle) County, Virginia

PARENTS: Peter and Jane Randolph Jefferson

FIRST LADY: None. (Jefferson's wife, Martha Wayles
Skelton Jefferson, known as Patsy, died nineteen years
before Jefferson was elected president. Jefferson's
oldest daughter, also named Patsy, acted as
hostess. Dolley Madison also helped out.)

KIDS: Martha Washington (also called Patsy,
after her mom), Jane Randolph, infant son
(born and died 1777), Lucy Elizabeth (1780–1781),
and Lucy Elizabeth Jefferson (1782–1785).
There are rumors that Jefferson was the father
of several other children by Sally Hemings.

COLLEGE: College of William and Mary

JOBS BEFORE PRESIDENT: Farmer, Lawyer,
Member of House of Burgesses,
Continental Congressman, Inventor

POLITICAL PARTY: Democratic-Republican

RELIGION: Deism

AGE AT INAUGURATION: Fifty-seven

YEARS IN OFFICE: 1801–1809

NICKNAME: Father of the Declaration of Independence

DIED: July 4, 1826

Thomas Jefferson

#3

—was the third president of the United States and probably one of the busiest! This guy was up before 5 A.M. to study things like zoology, agriculture, botany, and religion. After 8 A.M. he moved on to politics and law, and by the afternoon he was studying history. After this he usually took a two-mile run in the country, practiced his violin for three hours, and wound down each night reading literature and studying languages. And he somehow had time to invent the swivel chair, the folding ladder, the pedometer, a letter copier, and a walking stick that converted into a chair.

Jefferson was also responsible for some of our yummiest foods, like waffles, macaroni and cheese, and French fries. He was a farmer ahead of his time, producing crops of tomatoes (which people were afraid to eat, fearing they were poisonous), oranges, rice, garlic, and grapes for making wine. He also grew marijuana (but relax, because this founding father didn't inhale—the hemp in the marijuana plant was used for making clothes).

Thomas Jefferson considered writing the Declaration of Independence his greatest life achievement . . . and who wouldn't? Have you read it? When you think about it, it is a pretty big deal. The University of Virginia, which Jefferson founded, was also near and dear to his heart.

Thomas Jefferson's gravestone in Monticello (which he also designed!) reads:

> *Here was buried Thomas Jefferson,*
> *author of the Declaration of American Independence,*
> *of the statute of Virginia for religious freedom,*
> *and father of the University of Virginia*

Do you notice anything missing? Like . . . *president of the United States of America?*

Did You Know That . . .

★ Jefferson was a self-taught architect who designed and built his own estate, Monticello?

★ Jefferson wrote the Declaration of Independence in his early thirties?

★ Jefferson made two speeches during his entire presidency? (His two inauguration speeches.)

★ President Jefferson approved the Lewis and Clark Expedition?

★ Thomas Jefferson is the president with the most living descendants?

★ Jefferson bought the Louisiana Territory from France for four cents an acre? (Louisiana Purchase—$15,000,000.)

★ Jefferson had two grizzly bears given to him by Lewis and Clark? (He kept them on the White House lawn in cages.)

★ Thomas Jefferson entered the White House design contest under an "aka" name and was upset when he lost the competition?

★ Jefferson suffered regular migraine headaches?

★ Jefferson replaced the formal presidential bow with a regular handshake?

★ Jefferson designated "The President's Own" Marine Band, which still plays at most White House state functions, including inaugurations?

★ Thomas Jefferson served the very first French fries in the United States? (Thanks!)

★ Thomas Jefferson trained his pet mockingbird, Dick, to sing along as he played the violin?

★ The first baby to be born in the White House was James Madison Randolph, President Jefferson's grandson?

★ Thomas Jefferson was also responsible for bringing waffles to America? (He learned how to make them in the Netherlands.)

★ Thomas Jefferson founded the Democratic Party?

★ Jefferson did a really weird thing to ward off colds—he soaked his feet each morning in cold water?

★ Jefferson was responsible for the very first inaugural parade? (When he was walking back from the swearing-in ceremony, people began following him.)

★ Jefferson was fluent in four different languages? (Greek, English, Latin, and French.)

★ Jefferson also introduced macaroni and ice cream to America? (Thanks again!)

★ President Jefferson ran up a wine bill of over $10,000 during his term of office?

★ Jefferson many times greeted White House visitors wearing his pajamas and slippers?

★ Thomas Jefferson had his own vice president, Aaron Burr, arrested because Burr was secretly planning to form a new nation and break off from the United States?

★ Jefferson's favorite subject was math?

★ Jefferson's wife, Martha, supposedly asked him not to remarry when she died? (He didn't.)

★ The Library of Congress was made up of more than 6,000 of Thomas Jefferson's personally owned books? (He sold them for $23,900 to help start the Library of Congress.)

★ Jefferson died on July 4, 1826, on the fiftieth anniversary of the Declaration of Independence? (The same day as John Adams.)

★ Jefferson designed the University of Virginia?

★ Jefferson was the first president to be inaugurated in Washington, D.C.?

★ Jefferson's right hand was damaged permanently when he had an accident jumping over a fence trying to impress a girl? (He caught his foot and fell, hurting his hand.)

★ Jefferson lobbied against slavery his whole life, yet owned many slaves himself?

★ One of Jefferson's slaves, Sally Hemings, was the half sister of his wife, Martha Jefferson? (Sally was the daughter of Martha's dad and a slave woman.)

★ After his wife, Martha, died, Jefferson had a romance with Sally Hemings? (The press tried to turn this romance into a scandal. Jefferson never acknowledged or denied it.)

★ Jefferson tried to sell his home in a lottery to pay all of his debts when he was eighty-three years old?

★ President Jefferson's pet total was two dogs, eight birds, two bears, and nine horses?

★ When Thomas Jefferson became president he was given a 1,235-pound block of cheese? ("The greatest cheese in America for the greatest man in America" was carved into the side.)

★ The population of the United States when Jefferson was president was over 5 million?

★ Jefferson kept a notebook and pencils in his pocket so that he could always write down ideas?

★ President Jefferson was six feet two inches tall?

★ Jefferson's eyes were a hazel color?

BIRTHDAY: March 16, 1751,
in Port Conway, Virginia

PARENTS: James and Eleanor Rose Conway Madison

FIRST LADY: Dolley Payne Todd

KID: Payne Todd (Dolley was widowed
in her first marriage and this was her son)

COLLEGE: College of New Jersey
(now Princeton University)

JOBS BEFORE PRESIDENT: Politician,
Continental Congressman, Secretary of State
under Thomas Jefferson, Farmer

POLITICAL PARTY: Democratic-Republican

RELIGION: Episcopalian

AGE AT INAUGURATION: Fifty-seven

YEARS IN OFFICE: 1809–1817

NICKNAME: Father of the Constitution

DIED: June 28, 1836

James Madison

#4

—our smallest president, weighed in at a whopping 100 pounds and stood only five feet four inches tall. Apparently the British needed to pick on someone their own size, because so far James Madison is our only president to have faced enemy fire. It was the War of 1812, and it was going so poorly that he took command of a militia battery outside Washington. Despite this little guy's efforts we lost the war and the British actually ended up setting the White House on fire.

Picture this! Dolley Madison has prepared a nice home-cooked meal and has just placed it on the table for her family. She hears a knock at the door and panics when she realizes who it is . . . *the British*! With torches in hand, the British are ready to burn the White House. Dolley Madison makes history by scurrying around gathering up all the valuables she wants to save. As she slips out the back, the British sit down to her home-cooked meal before torching the White House. One of Dolley's historical saves is the official portrait of George Washington.

Determining the course of history, James Madison authored our Constitution and fought to add the Bill of Rights to this great document. Though he inherited some major problems when he became president, he did his best not to allow the unsuccessful war to define his presidency. But it did!

Did You Know That . . .

★ Madison's wife, Dolley, introduced ice cream to the White House?

★ Madison was the first president to wear long pants?

★ James Madison was the first congressman to become president?

★ Madison was the first president in history to ask Congress for a declaration of war?

★ Dolley Madison was taller than her husband?

★ Madison was the first president to be driven from the White House?

★ "The Star-Spangled Banner" was written during Madison's administration?

★ Madison graduated from the College of New Jersey (Princeton) in two years?

★ James Madison was the former secretary of state under Thomas Jefferson?

★ Madison was the youngest member of the Continental Congress?

★ The Executive Mansion became known as the White House during Madison's term?

★ Dolley Madison started the very first Easter Egg Roll on the Capitol grounds?

★ The first presidential inaugural ball was held during James Madison's inauguration?

★ Madison usually dressed in only black?

★ Dolley Madison wore turbans, ostrich feathers, jewels, and lots of makeup?

★ First Lady Madison liked to chew tobacco and gamble?

★ Dolley Madison was the first person to send a message using Morse code, in 1844?

★ Dolley Madison was given the highest honor ever awarded to a president's widow? (She was voted a lifetime seat on the floor of the House of Representatives.)

★ Madison died of heart failure at age eighty-five?

★ Indiana became a state during James Madison's presidency?

★ President Madison studied the Bible a lot?

★ Former president Madison was turned down for a loan from the Bank of the United States when he was desperate for money?

★ Dolley Madison purchased a piano for the White House?

★ Madison's nose had a scar on it from frostbite?

★ President Madison liked to read Greek and Latin?

★ President Madison was related to FDR?

★ James Madison was the only president who had two vice presidents die in office?

★ Madison became president of the University of Virginia after leaving office?

★ Madison was diagnosed with epilepsy by his doctors?

★ ★ ★ ★ ★ ★ ★ ★ ★ ★ ★ ★ ★ ★ ★ ★

Presidents Who Were U.S. Senators First

JAMES MONROE: Virginia

JOHN QUINCY ADAMS: Massachusetts

ANDREW JACKSON: Tennessee

MARTIN VAN BUREN: New York

WILLIAM HENRY HARRISON: Ohio

JOHN TYLER: Virginia

FRANKLIN PIERCE: New Hampshire

JAMES BUCHANAN: Pennsylvania

ANDREW JOHNSON: Tennessee

BENJAMIN HARRISON: Indiana

WARREN HARDING: Ohio

HARRY TRUMAN: Missouri

JOHN F. KENNEDY: Massachusetts

LYNDON B. JOHNSON: Texas

RICHARD NIXON: California

BIRTHDAY: April 28, 1758,
in Westmoreland County, Virginia

PARENTS: Spence and Elizabeth Jones Monroe

FIRST LADY: Elizabeth Kortright

KIDS: Eliza Kortright, James Spence (1799–1800),
and Maria Hester Monroe

COLLEGE: College of William and Mary

JOBS BEFORE PRESIDENT: Farmer, Soldier,
Lawyer, Continental Congressman, U.S. Senator,
Diplomat, Governor of Virginia, Secretary of State
and Secretary of War under James Madison

POLITICAL PARTY: Democratic-Republican

RELIGION: Episcopalian

AGE AT INAUGURATION: Fifty-eight

YEARS IN OFFICE: 1817–1825

NICKNAME: Last Cocked Hat

DIED: July 4, 1831

James Monroe

#5

—was the last of the Revolutionary leaders to hold office. Because the White House was under construction, Monroe toured the country and visited with Americans. The Monroes sold the government their own personal furniture and antiques just to get the White House up and running again for the annual New Year's reception in 1818. Remember, everything had been burned and destroyed by the British in 1812.

He established the Monroe Doctrine, which warned other countries to stay off North and South American soil. His presidency is remembered for this great document, though he did not write a word of it.

Monroe was wounded during the Revolutionary War and carried the souvenir bullet in his shoulder the rest of his life. Monroe was the only president to serve as both secretary of state and secretary of war at the same time. In his earlier days he was known as a bit of a rebel because he voted against ratifying the Constitution and once defied orders from George Washington himself and lost his job as minister to France.

He spoke fluent French and actually preferred it to speaking English. His daughter was the first child of a president to marry in the White House. Her name was Maria Hester Monroe. His presidency was known as "the Era of Good Feelings" and his popularity gained him another term with no opponents whatsoever.

Did You Know That . . .

★ Monroe wanted to return slaves to Africa?

★ James Monroe was the only U.S. president who had a foreign capital named after him? (Monrovia, Liberia.)

★ Monroe was one of three presidents who died on July 4? (1831.)

★ Monroe was the first president to ride a steamboat? (The *Savannah*, in 1819.)

★ Monroe held more offices than any other president? (Senator; governor; minister to Britain, France, and Spain; secretary of state; and secretary of war.)

★ Monroe went to college at age sixteen?

★ Monroe received every electoral vote except one? (The delegate who cast his vote for the opponent wanted George Washington to be the only president to receive every electoral vote.)

★ President Monroe was unopposed for reelection in 1820?

★ President Monroe once chased his secretary of the treasury out of the White House with a set of fire tongs during a disagreement?

★ Congress made the official number of stripes on the American flag thirteen, to represent the thirteen colonies, during Monroe's administration?

★ Monroe purchased Florida from Spain?

★ Monroe was the last president to wear a powdered wig?

★ Monroe was the last president to wear short pants? (Even though Madison wore long ones.)

★ President Monroe stayed in the White House three weeks after leaving office because his wife was sick and couldn't be moved?

★ Monroe was the first president who had been a senator?

★ President Monroe tried to get his cabinet members to wear uniforms? (Never worked.)

★ President Monroe once broke up a fight at a White House dinner between the British and French ministers?

★ Missouri became a state while Monroe was president?

★ Monroe was always broke and died penniless?

★ Monroe and his wife held a weekly tea at the White House?

★ Monroe was just over six feet tall?

★ President Monroe had dark wavy hair and blue-gray eyes?

★ James Monroe liked to ride horses and hunt?

★ President Monroe once signed a petition as a college student that complained about the food? (There wasn't enough and it was awful.)

★ James Monroe was given a pair of sheepdogs as a gift from Frenchman Marquis de Lafayette?

★ ★ ★ ★ ★ ★ ★ ★ ★ ★ ★ ★ ★ ★ ★

Presidents Who Were Vice Presidents First

JOHN ADAMS

THOMAS JEFFERSON

MARTIN VAN BUREN

JOHN TYLER

MILLARD FILLMORE

ANDREW JOHNSON

CHESTER ARTHUR

THEODORE ROOSEVELT

CALVIN COOLIDGE

HARRY TRUMAN

LYNDON B. JOHNSON

RICHARD NIXON

GERALD FORD

GEORGE H. W. BUSH

BIRTHDAY: July 11, 1767, in Braintree
(now Quincy), Massachusetts

PARENTS: John and Abigail Smith Adams

FIRST LADY: Louisa Catherine Johnson

KIDS: George Washington, John, Charles Francis,
and Louisa Catherine Adams

COLLEGE: Harvard

JOBS BEFORE PRESIDENT: Lawyer, Foreign Minister,
Secretary of State under James Monroe

POLITICAL PARTY: Democratic-Republican

RELIGION: Unitarian

AGE AT INAUGURATION: Fifty-seven

YEARS IN OFFICE: 1825–1829

NICKNAME: Old Man Eloquent

DIED: February 23, 1848

John Quincy Adams

#6

—entered office riding a horse named *Scandal*. His horse was not really named Scandal, but he did enter the presidency as part of a huge political scandal that would follow him right out of office after only one term. Does history repeat itself or what?

The election of 1824 was the first election in history not to have a clear winner. Neither candidate received enough electoral votes, so the House of Representatives had to decide. There had been four candidates running for the job. The Constitution allowed the top three to go to the House for a decision. Mysteriously, the fourth candidate was already the Speaker of the House. The selection was made, and John Quincy Adams was the winner. Here is the scandalous part: John Quincy Adams chose the Speaker of the House as his secretary of state. Was there wheeling and dealing going on here? History decided probably so. This made his administration totally ineffective.

Though he was short and fat, this didn't stop Adams from being a star swimmer. He swam nude in the Potomac River each morning. Have you seen this river? Have you been to Washington, D.C., in the wintertime? Enough said.

Adams would strip off his clothes and jump into the icy waters of the Potomac for his daily swim. Sometimes people would steal his clothes or use them to get what they wanted from him. On one occasion President Adams had to beg a schoolboy to run all the way to the White House and get him some more clothes. In this case there was no dirty political laundry to air.

Did You Know That . . .

★ Adams had a pet alligator, which he kept in the East Room bathtub of the White House?

★ Adams was the first president to have a father who had been president? (John Adams.)

★ John Quincy Adams was the first president to be an expert pool/billiards player?

★ Louisa Johnson Adams was the only foreign First Lady?

★ President Adams read the Bible from cover to cover each year?

★ Adams was the only president to be elected to the House of Representatives *after* being president?

★ Adams was the first president to use a telescope in the White House? (He loved astronomy.)

★ John Quincy Adams was the only president to be interviewed naked? (A reporter withheld Adams's clothes during his morning Potomac swim in the buff and promised to give them back in return for an interview.)

★ Adams was the only president to use ice water in the White House bathtub? (He would also scrub himself during his chilly bath with a horsehair mitt until his skin was raw.)

★ John Quincy Adams was the first president to have his picture taken (before taking office)?

★ From age eleven, John Quincy was his dad's private secretary? (His dad was an American diplomat in Russia before being president.)

★ Adams watched the Battle of Bunker Hill as a little boy?

★ John Quincy Adams loved to garden?

★ John Quincy Adams said, "The four most miserable years of my life were my four years in the presidency"?

★ Adams was the first and only president to be published as a poet?

★ Adams was the only former president to have suffered a fatal stroke on the House floor? (He was giving an antislavery speech; he was eighty.)

★ Adams was the first president to have and use a middle name?

★ President Adams loved wine?

★ Adams was an early riser, sometimes getting up before 4 A.M., and went to bed close to midnight?

★ John Quincy Adams was a sloppy dresser and wore the same old hat for ten years?

★ Adams wrote in his diary each day from age seventeen until his death?

★ First Lady Louisa Adams wrote a play called *Suspicion* in the year 1826?

★ Adams's personality got on people's nerves? (He was annoying.)

★ Two of Adams's three sons were alcoholics and one committed suicide?

★ Adams was five feet seven inches tall and weighed 175 pounds?

★ John Quincy Adams actually wrote the Monroe Doctrine?

★ ★ ★ ★ ★ ★ ★ ★ ★ ★ ★ ★ ★ ★ ★ ★

The White House Contains . . .

1	Tennis Court	3	Elevators
1	Swimming Pool	28	Fireplaces
1	Movie Theater	132	Rooms
1	Jogging Track	35	Bathrooms
6	Stories	412	Doors
8	Staircases	147	Windows

- There are 6,300 pieces of crystal in each East Room chandelier.
- The South Portico was added in 1824 and the North Portico in 1830.
- The president's private movie theater is located between the White House and the East Wing.
- Eight hundred ninety-five gallons of paint were used on the inside of the White House during the remodeling of 1949–52.
- Nine hundred ten tons of structural and reinforcement steel were added to the White House during the remodeling of 1949–52.
- The White House receives over one and a half million visitors annually.
- The White House architect was James Hoban.
- The first cornerstone-laying of the White House occurred on October 13, 1792.
- President John Adams was the first occupant of the White House.

BIRTHDAY: March 15, 1767,
in Waxhaw, South Carolina

PARENTS: Andrew and Elizabeth Hutchinson Jackson

FIRST LADY: Rachel Donelson Robards

KID: Andrew (adopted)

COLLEGE: None

JOBS BEFORE PRESIDENT: Soldier, Lawyer,
Congressman, U.S. Senator, Judge, Governor of Florida

POLITICAL PARTY: Democratic

RELIGION: Presbyterian

AGE AT INAUGURATION: Sixty-one

YEARS IN OFFICE: 1829–1837

NICKNAME: Old Hickory

DIED: June 8, 1845

Andrew Jackson

#7

—insisted that the world was flat. This persistent hotheadedness was exactly why people were willing to follow his leadership. He was one of our most popular presidents and an entire era is named for him, "the Age of Jackson." In 1835 Jackson eliminated the national debt, for the first and only time in our history.

Jackson is possibly the only president to have a debate over his birthplace. He was born in a log cabin near Waxhaw. The boundary between the states is too close to call, so both North Carolina and South Carolina claim him. He believed that he was born in South Carolina.

Many people today would classify Jackson as insane. Serving in two wars didn't help his personality. His crazy behavior was cause for concern. For instance, he would purposely get into arguments and fights with others. He always sought extreme revenge. His insanity was possibly due to breathing a few too many cannonball fumes.

He was as tough as nails and some called him Old Hickory. Though strong and belligerent, he had constant headaches, stomach problems, and a nagging cough. He had lots of battle scars and two souvenir bullets lodged inside him. He had one removed with absolutely no anesthesia and the other remained. Jackson is the only known U.S. president to have participated in over 100 duels. In one bloody duel, he shot and killed a man named Charles Dickinson for insulting his wife, Rachel.

Jackson insisted that the White House belonged to the people and that they should have access to it whenever they pleased. After his inauguration he invited the public to the White House to celebrate. Crowds came by the hundreds. They were so unruly and obnoxious that Jackson escaped through a window and spent the night in a hotel.

This president had a very colorful vocabulary (if you know what I mean). His pet parrot, Poll, picked up on this bad habit and cursed constantly. When the president died, the bird had to be removed from Jackson's funeral for sharing its colorful vocabulary (again, if you know what I mean!).

Did You Know That . . .

★ Andrew Jackson was the first president to have an assassination attempt on his life?

★ Jackson joined the army at age thirteen?

★ The capital of Mississippi (Jackson) is named for him?

★ Jackson was the first president to ride on a train? (After being president.)

★ President Jackson was our only known "dueling" president?

★ Andrew Jackson was the first president to be born in a log cabin?

★ Jackson was the very last Revolutionary War veteran to become president?

★ Andrew Jackson was a practical joker in his youth? (He liked to move people's outhouses in the night to where they could not find them.)

★ Jackson stood six feet tall and never weighed more than 145 pounds?

★ Jackson had rotten teeth?

★ Andrew Jackson was the only president to have been a prisoner of war? (American Revolution.)

★ Jackson was the only president to have served in both the Revolutionary War and the War of 1812?

★ Andrew Jackson was the only president to marry his wife twice?

★ Jackson's wife died before his inauguration?

★ President Jackson kept his racehorses in the stables at the White House? (He loved to gamble on them in races.)

★ During Jackson's presidency, running water and bathrooms were added to the White House?

★ President Jackson had an unofficial group of advisers who were more important to him than his cabinet? (This group was known as "the Kitchen Cabinet.")

★ Andrew Jackson purchased a piano and twenty spittoons for the White House?

★ Jackson was the first president to be nominated by a political party?

★ As a little boy, Jackson would read the newspaper to illiterate townspeople and talk with them?

★ Andrew Jackson suffered smallpox as a child?

★ President Jackson's mom died when he was fourteen?

★ Andrew Jackson rewarded friends and supporters with government jobs? (This didn't turn out so well.)

★ Arkansas became a state while Jackson was president?

★ The typewriter was invented while Jackson was president?

★ Jackson raised eleven children in his lifetime even though none of them were his? (He loved children and took several in.)

★ Andrew Jackson had a permanent scar on his forehead? (A British soldier forced thirteen-year-old Jackson to clean his boots and he refused, so the soldier slashed his forehead.)

★ The population of the United States when Andrew Jackson was leaving office was almost 16 million?

★ Jackson was the first president in history to have a cabinet nominee rejected?

★ President Jackson had a disability in childhood that made him slobber all the time?

★ Andrew Jackson left the White House with only $90 in his pocket, and that was literally all he had?

★ Jackson was often referred to as the first "frontier president"?

★ Andrew Jackson once served a 1,400-pound block of cheddar cheese as a snack at an open-house party held in the White House? (The guests consumed all 1,400 pounds of cheese in 2 hours.)

BIRTHDAY: December 5, 1782,
in Kinderhook, New York

PARENTS: Abraham and Maria Hoes Van Alen Van Buren

FIRST LADY: Hannah Hoes

KIDS: Abraham, John, Martin, Winfield Scott,
and Smith Thompson Van Buren

COLLEGE: None

JOBS BEFORE PRESIDENT: Lawyer, New York
State Senator, U.S. Senator, Governor of New York,
Secretary of State and Vice President
under Andrew Jackson

POLITICAL PARTY: Democratic

RELIGION: Dutch Reformed

AGE AT INAUGURATION: Fifty-four

YEARS IN OFFICE: 1837–1841

NICKNAMES: Little Magician;
Old Kinderhook (O.K.); the Red Fox

DIED: July 24, 1862

Martin Van Buren

#8

—was often called the Little Magician for his skill and wit and for being the main man responsible for organizing the Democratic Party. With this type of résumé, you would think that Van Buren would have the greatest term ever. Sadly, this magician ran out of tricks when he entered office. The fault was not his entirely. He had inherited the financial mess that Andrew Jackson had created with the Bank War, which eventually led to the Panic of 1837. He avoided addressing the panic and dealing with it swiftly, which led to an even worse second depression in 1839. He never personally or politically recovered from this and was defeated in reelection.

These depressions did not affect his love of "the finer things in life," which seemed to anger the public. Van Buren *loved* to dress in fine clothes and ride in the most elegant carriages available. Because of his taste for "the good life," the American people perceived that he did not care about them or their impossible situation. He became one of the most unpopular presidents of all time.

Not to mention one final act that probably sealed his fate for sure: He opposed statehood for Texas. If he had just known that you *"don't mess with Texas"* and get away with it!

Did You Know That . . .

★ Van Buren was sometimes called Old Kinderhook? (Referring to his birthplace.)

★ President Van Buren was sometimes referred to as the Red Fox because of his red hair?

★ Old Kinderhook became "O.K." during the election, referring to Van Buren as a trusted candidate who was "okay"?

★ Van Buren was the first president born in America after it declared independence?

★ President Van Buren's parents were Dutch immigrants?

★ Martin Van Buren enjoyed drinking wine?

★ Van Buren was responsible for painting the Blue Room blue?

★ Van Buren grew potato plants during his retirement?

★ Martin Van Buren had no facial hair but did have sideburns?

★ President Van Buren enjoyed going to the theater and opera?

★ Van Buren's son Abraham was his personal secretary?

★ President Van Buren left instructions for no bells to be rung during his funeral?

★ Martin Van Buren married his childhood sweetheart and first cousin, Hannah Hoes?

★ Martin Van Buren was the first president to campaign like we do now, with speeches, fund-raisers, and rallies?

★ Van Buren was the first president born after the Declaration of Independence?

★ President Van Buren was criticized by the public for refurnishing the White House and using golden spoons?

★ At age sixty-eight Van Buren was turned down when he proposed marriage? (Margaret Sylvester, age forty.)

★ Van Buren was the first president to have more than one inaugural ball because of the high demand for tickets?

★ President Van Buren was five feet six inches tall?

★ Martin Van Buren had wiry white hair and blue eyes?

★ Van Buren wore side-whiskers?

★ Martin Van Buren was an optimist?

★ Martin Van Buren's father owned a tavern that Martin worked in as a kid?

BIRTHDAY: February 9, 1773,
in Charles City County, Virginia

PARENTS: Benjamin and Elizabeth Bassett Harrison

FIRST LADY: Anna Tuthill Symmes

KIDS: Elizabeth Bassett, John Cleves Symmes,
Lucy Singleton, William Henry, John Scott, Benjamin,
Mary Symmes, Carter Bassett, Anna Tuthill,
and James Findlay (1814–1817) Harrison

COLLEGE: Hampden-Sydney College

JOBS BEFORE PRESIDENT: Soldier, Governor of
Indiana Territory, Congressman, Ohio State Senator,
U.S. Senator, Minister to Colombia

POLITICAL PARTY: Whig

RELIGION: Episcopalian

AGE AT INAUGURATION: Sixty-eight

YEAR IN OFFICE: 1841 (thirty days)

NICKNAME: Old Tippecanoe

DIED: April 4, 1841

William Henry Harrison
#9

—was sixty-eight years old when he took office. You would think that he would have listened to his mom, who most likely told him once if she told him a thousand times to put on his coat, hat, and gloves when going out in the cold to play. Well, he obviously didn't remember her warnings.

He had been tired of the press and others calling him old and simple during the campaign and decided to show them a thing or two. His intent was to give a long and scholarly inaugural speech. He succeeded in the "long" part, but it is questionable about the "scholarly" part. You can't be too scholarly if you give the longest inaugural speech in history (almost two hours in length) on the coldest, dampest, windiest, chilliest day of the year without a coat or a hat or at least some gloves.

Everyone who attended the inauguration was dressed for the cold with coats and hats, just not President Harrison. By setting a record for longest inaugural speech in history, he would unintentionally set another record. William Henry Harrison is the only president to have served only one month in office. Due to the fact that he was standing out in the cold for so long with no protection, he caught a cold that turned into pneumonia and he died one month after his inauguration.

The moral of this story is: Keep it short! Oh, and listen to your mother!

Did You Know That . . .

★ William Henry Harrison was the first president to have gone to medical school?

★ Harrison's dad was a signer of the Declaration of Independence and a friend of George Washington's?

★ Harrison was a war hero?

★ Harrison was retired when asked to run for president by the Whigs?

★ William Harrison did the family shopping? (Seriously!)

★ Harrison had a cow named Sukey?

★ President Harrison was very religious and refused to discuss politics on Sundays?

★ William Harrison was one of ten presidents to have served less than one term in office?

★ William Henry Harrison was the grandfather of a future president? (Benjamin Harrison.)

★ Harrison was the first president elected from the Whig Party?

★ Harrison and his vice president, John Tyler, were referred to as the "fertility ticket"? (When they ran for office, they'd had twenty-five children between them—ten for Harrison and fifteen for Tyler.)

★ President Harrison loved to drink hard cider?

★ Harrison used a log cabin symbol in his campaign but was not born in a log cabin and never lived in one? (Hmmmm.)

★ William Harrison's inaugural speech contained 8,445 words? (Huh!)

★ Harrison was the first president to be photographed in office?

★ Harrison was the only president born in the same county as his vice president?

★ Harrison was the first president to die in office?

★ Anna, Harrison's wife, received a $25,000 pension after his death?

★ Harrison was the first of three presidents named William?

★ Harrison was the first president to lie in state at the White House? (East Room.)

★ President Harrison was of average height and slim?

★ When Harrison was a child, his home was attacked during the American Revolution and all furnishings, belongings, and livestock were taken?

★ Harrison attended the University of Pennsylvania Medical School but never graduated?

BIRTHDAY: March 29, 1790, in Greenway, Virginia

PARENTS: John and Mary Marot Armistead Tyler

FIRST LADIES: Letitia Christian and Julia Gardiner

KIDS: Mary, Robert, John, Letitia, Elizabeth,
Ann Contesse (born and died 1825), Alice, Tazewell,
David Gardiner, John Alexander, Julia Gardiner,
Lachlan, Lyon Gardiner, Robert Fitzwalter,
and Pearl Tyler

COLLEGE: College of William and Mary

JOBS BEFORE PRESIDENT: Soldier, Lawyer,
Governor of Virginia, U.S. Senator, Vice President
under William Henry Harrison

POLITICAL PARTY: Whig

RELIGION: Episcopalian

AGE AT INAUGURATION: Fifty-one

YEARS IN OFFICE: 1841–1845

NICKNAME: His Accidency

DIED: January 18, 1862

John Tyler

#10

—assumed office when President William Henry Harrison died. He was playing marbles with his kids when he got the news that he was to be sworn in. A president had never died before and no one knew how to handle the situation. Most people, including the cabinet, began referring to Tyler as His Accidency because he was the president "by accident." They believed that he would just be a substitute and make no big decisions or choices. John Tyler had ideas of his own. He began his administration by refusing to open a letter that was addressed to "the Acting President." By his standing up and truly becoming the president, he angered the cabinet, which had planned to make all the decisions for him. His party ultimately disowned him and he became the first president without a party.

President Tyler had enjoyed a twenty-nine-year marriage to his wife Letitia Tyler. They had seven children together. His wife suffered a stroke and died his second year in office. She was the first First Lady to die in the White House. President Tyler was devastated but most likely needed help with his seven kids. He was happy to find new love and married Julia Gardiner. First Lady Julia Gardiner Tyler was very much in love with Tyler despite the fact that he was fifty-three and she was twenty-three. She was musical, festive, and full of life. They had eight children together, bringing Tyler's total to fifteen, the most of any president. Julia was younger than Tyler's first three children.

The Tylers were so happy in their new life that they wanted everyone to be happy, including their pet canary named Johnny Ty. Julia wrote to her family to find their canary a mate. Soon they received a shipment from New York. Everyone was thrilled to see a beautiful canary that would make Johnny Ty's life as happy as theirs was. Johnny Ty seemed so excited when they put the other bird in his cage with him. He was very happy. Then, without warning, Johnny jumped off his perch and sat at the bottom of the cage. Days later he was dead. What could have happened? When the Tylers investigated, they found out the new bird was also a male. *Ooooops!*

Tyler ultimately defined the course of action when a president dies . . . and when a canary does, too!

Did You Know That . . .

★ All of President Tyler's cabinet quit except for one man?

★ John Tyler fired his son as his press secretary for drinking too much?

★ Tyler was the great-uncle of Harry S. Truman?

★ Tyler was the first president to have a veto overridden?

★ Tyler had a beloved horse named General?

★ President Tyler had a greyhound dog named Le Beau?

★ Five years after leaving the White House Tyler was penniless?

★ Tyler was the first president to marry while in office? (Second marriage.)

★ Julia Tyler is the only known First Lady to wear a forehead jewel?

★ First Lady Julia Tyler introduced America to the polka? (She loved dancing.)

★ President Tyler was a violinist and his wife Julia played guitar?

★ Almost twenty years after his presidency, Tyler joined the Confederacy?

★ Tyler was the only former president to be named a "sworn enemy of the United States"? (For joining the Confederacy.)

★ A city in the state of Texas was named for John Tyler? (Tyler, Texas—the year after Tyler left office, in 1846.)

★ Texas joined the Union on Tyler's last day in office?

★ President Tyler was buried in New York, then exhumed and re-interred in Virginia?

★ John Tyler was the only former U.S. president elected to the Confederate Congress? (He died before he could serve.)

★ Julia Tyler began the tradition of the Marine Band playing "Hail to the Chief" when the president entered the room at state functions? (This continues today.)

★ Florida became the twenty-seventh state in the United States during Tyler's presidency?

★ Tyler's granddaughter, named Letitia after her grandmother, was the first girl born in the White House?

★ President Tyler died at age seventy-one? (Only a year and a half after his youngest, and fifteenth, child was born.)

★ Tyler was the first president to have federally funded security at the White House? (Four men in plain clothes at the door.)

★ John Tyler was the only known president to stand up to an angry mob that was protesting at the White House?

★ Tyler was a supporter of science and the arts?

★ Tyler was born during George Washington's term?

★ ★ ★ ★ ★ ★ ★ ★ ★ ★ ★ ★ ★ ★ ★ ★

The Top 10 Presidential Electoral Vote Totals

10. Dwight Eisenhower: 442 (1952)

9. Herbert Hoover: 444 (1928)

8. Franklin D. Roosevelt: 449 (1940)

7. Dwight Eisenhower: 457 (1956)

6. Franklin D. Roosevelt: 472 (1932)

5. Lyndon Johnson: 486 (1964)

4. Ronald Reagan: 489 (1980)

3. Richard Nixon: 520 (1972)

2. Franklin D. Roosevelt: 523 (1936)

1. Ronald Reagan: 525 (1984)

BIRTHDAY: November 2, 1795,
in Pineville, North Carolina

PARENTS: Samuel and Jane Knox Polk

FIRST LADY: Sarah Childress

KIDS: None

COLLEGE: University of North Carolina

JOBS BEFORE PRESIDENT: Soldier, Lawyer,
Congressman, Speaker of the House,
Governor of Tennessee

POLITICAL PARTY: Democratic

RELIGION: Presbyterian and Methodist

AGE AT INAUGURATION: Forty-nine

YEARS IN OFFICE: 1845–1849

NICKNAME: Young Hickory

DIED: June 15, 1849

James K. Polk

#11

—was the "dark horse" candidate for his party. He became the president because of his stand on expanding the United States and because Martin Van Buren was the other choice. While in office he made decisions that were influenced by what Andrew Jackson thought, earning him the nickname Young Hickory. Despite his nickname, he was *very* different from Jackson in personality and leadership style.

He was not the wild host to hordes of folks at the White House that Jackson had been. In fact, he was quite the opposite. No parties, no drinking, no fooling around. Fun was not an option. He worked and did not play. His family did the same. His wife was his personal secretary while he was the president. Together they worked twelve to sixteen hours a day and slept very little.

During his four-year administration he was away from the White House for only six weeks total (on business, of course). During his presidency he took no vacations; he negotiated peace with Britain and presided over the controversial Mexican War, and was probably more than ready to step down when his four years were up.

Because of Polk's efforts and the territory gained in the Mexican War, the United States finally stretched from sea to shining sea (hey . . . isn't that a song?). He died three months after leaving the White House. Some say he died from sheer exhaustion and overwork. Maybe he died because he never had fun. Either way, you know what they say: "All work and no play makes for a very dull boy," or tired one!

Did You Know That . . .

★ James Polk bought land from Mexico that would eventually be Nevada, California, New Mexico, some of Colorado, Arizona, Wyoming, and Utah?

★ Polk was president during the gold rush in California?

★ Polk and his wife hosted the very first formal Thanksgiving dinner ever in the White House?

★ James Polk owned slaves?

★ President Polk didn't trust the banks and kept his money stashed at home?

★ President and Mrs. Polk were personal friends of Francis Scott Key? (He wrote "The Star-Spangled Banner.")

★ Polk was one of only three presidents who had no children?

★ Polk made five campaign promises and fulfilled them all in four years?

★ James Polk was the first "dark horse" candidate?

★ Election Day was set during Polk's term? (The first Tuesday after the first Monday in November.)

★ The first gaslights were installed in the White House during Polk's administration?

★ President Polk was five feet eight inches tall?

★ Polk signed the bill that created the Smithsonian Institution?

★ James Polk was the first president to voluntarily serve only one term?

★ First Lady Sarah Polk lived forty-two years after President Polk died?

★ Postage stamps were introduced during Polk's presidency?

★ James Polk was the only president to have been Speaker of the House?

★ Polk had gallstone surgery at age seventeen with no anesthesia?

★ Polk was the first president to have his inaugural address sent out by telegraph? (By Samuel Morse himself.)

★ Iowa and Texas were new states to the Union during Polk's administration?

★ Polk's family had been Presbyterian and he was baptized as a Methodist one week before his death?

★ Polk was president during the Mexican War? (Called "Mr. Polk's War.")

★ Polk asked Congress for permission to declare war on Mexico because it was unwilling to sell California?

★ The Polks were the first family to use an icebox in the White House?

★ James Polk had gray eyes?

★ President Polk had long white hair that was combed back?

★ ★ ★ ★ ★ ★ ★ ★ ★ ★ ★ ★ ★ ★ ★ ★

Presidents Who Were Elected to Two Terms

GEORGE WASHINGTON

THOMAS JEFFERSON

JAMES MADISON

JAMES MONROE

ANDREW JACKSON

ABRAHAM LINCOLN

ULYSSES S. GRANT

GROVER CLEVELAND

WILLIAM MCKINLEY

WOODROW WILSON

DWIGHT EISENHOWER

RICHARD NIXON

RONALD REAGAN

BILL CLINTON

GEORGE W. BUSH

BIRTHDAY: November 24, 1784,
in Montebello, Virginia

PARENTS: Richard and Sarah Dabney Strother Taylor

FIRST LADY: Margaret Mackall Smith

KIDS: Ann Mackall, Sarah Knox,
Octavia Pannill (1816–1820),
Margaret Smith (1819–1820),
Mary Elizabeth, and Richard Taylor

COLLEGE: None

JOBS BEFORE PRESIDENT: Farmer, Soldier

POLITICAL PARTY: Whig

RELIGION: Episcopalian

AGE AT INAUGURATION: Sixty-four

YEARS IN OFFICE: 1849–1850

NICKNAME: Old Rough and Ready

DIED: July 9, 1850

Zachary Taylor
#12

—was not the shining example that you would expect to become president. He never went to school, he had no political experience, he never ran for any office, and the most surprising thing is that he had never, ever voted. Hello? He didn't even vote for himself in his own presidential election.

His biggest mistake as president was doing nothing about slavery. It seemed he was neither for it nor against it. Although he was a slave owner himself, Taylor was torn on the issue of slavery, and tensions were mounting between the North and the South. He never got to address those tensions because of a weird snack he ate.

At one hot, sweaty, sticky, humid, scorching (okay, so maybe it was too hot to be outside) Fourth of July celebration, President

Taylor sought relief from the heat. He needed something that would cool him off and satisfy his growling stomach. He reached for a bowl of cherries and then washed them down with some ice-cold milk. After five days of vomiting and diarrhea he died. Many believed that he had been poisoned with arsenic.

In 1991 his family had his body exhumed and examined. They found no evidence of arsenic and determined that he most likely died of cholera. What does all this ultimately prove? Life is *not* a bowl of cherries and milk *does not* always do a body good!

Did You Know That . . .

★ Zachary Taylor was a military general?

★ Taylor had to be boosted onto his horse?

★ Taylor was the second president to die in office?

★ Taylor dressed like a farmer rather than a president? (Even in the White House.)

★ Zachary Taylor was a second cousin of James Madison, fourth cousin once removed of Robert E. Lee, and fourth cousin three times removed of FDR? (What a connection!)

★ Taylor refused postage-due correspondence that notified him of his nomination for president? (So he didn't find out for a while.)

★ Whitney was President Taylor's famous warhorse? (The horse stayed perfectly still while Taylor stood up in the stirrups to allow a cannonball aimed at him to pass through his legs. The horse was hailed as a hero.)

★ When Taylor became president, Whitney was retired to graze on the most famous lawn in America, at the White House? (People would pluck hairs from his tail as souvenirs.)

★ His horse Whitney followed the president's funeral procession?

★ Taylor chewed tobacco and rarely missed when he spit in the White House spittoons?

★ Taylor was a horrible speller?

★ Taylor's daughter Sarah married Jefferson Davis, who became president of the Confederacy?

★ Abraham Lincoln gave Taylor's eulogy when he died?

★ Taylor was one of seven presidents from Virginia?

★ Taylor was one of six presidents born in a log cabin?

★ President Taylor was five feet eight inches tall and weighed about 200 pounds?

BIRTHDAY: January 7, 1800, in Locke Township (now Summerhill), New York

PARENTS: Nathaniel and Phoebe Millard Fillmore
Stepmother: Eunice Love

FIRST LADY: Abigail Powers
(1798–1853; she died right after his term ended)

KIDS: Millard Powers and Mary Abigail Fillmore

COLLEGE: None

JOBS BEFORE PRESIDENT: Soldier, Lawyer, Congressman, Vice President under Zachary Taylor

POLITICAL PARTY: Whig

RELIGION: Unitarian

AGE AT INAUGURATION: Fifty

YEARS IN OFFICE: 1850–1853

NICKNAME: The Compromise President

Died: March 8, 1874

Millard Fillmore

#13

—fell in love with his teacher. She also fell in love with him. This would make headlines in today's papers. Scandal? You be the judge. He started school later than most kids. Miss Powers felt sorry for Millard because he had taught himself to read but not very well. She improved his reading skills to the point that he developed a lifelong love of reading and owned over 4,000 books. She also taught him to write and spell while casting her own "spell" on him.

Miss Powers opened up a whole new world to him that he had never known. No, we are *not* going there and this is *not* the scandalous part.

Fillmore was nineteen and Abigail Powers was twenty-one when they fell in love. She inspired him to learn and he inspired her to teach. Because he had started school when he was eighteen, he felt he was behind and was extra eager to learn and catch up. Can you believe this future president had never seen a map of the United States until he was nineteen years old?

Fillmore was amiable and friendly, yet in charge. He reversed most of the decisions that Zachary Taylor had made, and when his cabinet gave him flak about it, he fired them all. He didn't even have a vice president. His road was not easy because he had assumed the presidency and not been elected to it. He supported slavery for economic reasons and signed the Compromise of 1850 into law. This made him very unpopular even with his own party. He was not nominated for a second term and went down in history as a "forgettable president."

Did You Know That . . .

★ First Lady Abigail Fillmore started the White House Library?

★ President Fillmore gave government money to establish the railroad from the East Coast to the West Coast in order to bring back the gold?

★ President Fillmore had been named for his mother, Phoebe Millard Fillmore?

★ Fillmore did not make an inaugural address?

★ Millard Fillmore was the last president born in the eighteenth century?

★ Fillmore was the first president to turn down an honorary degree? (Doctor of civil law from Oxford. He believed that you should not receive a degree that you cannot read or understand.)

★ Millard Fillmore became the chancellor at the University of Buffalo after leaving office?

★ Fillmore was born in a log cabin? (One of six presidents who were.)

★ Millard Fillmore was a member and former president of the Society for the Prevention of Cruelty to Animals, Buffalo, New York, chapter?

★ Fillmore's statue is in front of city hall in Buffalo, New York?

★ Fillmore was the second vice president in history to assume the presidency due to the death of a president?

★ Millard Fillmore and some of his cabinet helped to put a fire out at the Library of Congress?

★ California became a state during Fillmore's term as president?

★ After leaving office Fillmore ran as a candidate for the Know-Nothing Party, which wanted only American-born Protestants elected to public office? (He carried only one state.)

★ Millard Fillmore's eyes were blue?

★ The first kitchen stove was installed in the White House during his presidency?

★ President Fillmore was six feet tall?

★ Fillmore's hair was solid white when he was president?

★ Fillmore was apprenticed to a tailor by his father for three years?

★ Millard Fillmore did not smoke, drink, or gamble?

★ Fillmore was the second of nine children?

★ Fillmore's first wife died soon after his term ended? (She caught a cold that turned into pneumonia at Franklin Pierce's inauguration and died weeks later.)

★ ★ ★ ★ ★ ★ ★ ★ ★ ★ ★ ★ ★ ★ ★

Presidents Who Were Elected to Only One Term

JOHN ADAMS

JOHN QUINCY ADAMS

MARTIN VAN BUREN

WILLIAM HENRY HARRISON

JAMES POLK

ZACHARY TAYLOR

FRANKLIN PIERCE

JAMES BUCHANAN

RUTHERFORD B. HAYES

JAMES GARFIELD

BENJAMIN HARRISON

THEODORE ROOSEVELT

WILLIAM TAFT

WARREN HARDING

CALVIN COOLIDGE

HERBERT HOOVER

HARRY TRUMAN

JOHN F. KENNEDY

LYNDON B. JOHNSON

JIMMY CARTER

GEORGE H. W. BUSH

BIRTHDAY: November 23, 1804, in Hillsborough (now Hillsboro), New Hampshire

PARENTS: Benjamin and Ann Kendrick Pierce

FIRST LADY: Jane Means Appleton

KIDS: Franklin (born and died 1863), Frank Robert (1839–1843), and Benjamin (1841–1853) Pierce

COLLEGE: Bowdoin College

JOBS BEFORE PRESIDENT: Lawyer, Member of New Hampshire State Legislature, Congressman, U.S. Senator, Soldier

POLITICAL PARTY: Democratic

RELIGION: Episcopalian

AGE AT INAUGURATION: Forty-eight

YEARS IN OFFICE: 1853–1857

NICKNAMES: Fainting Frank; Handsome Frank

DIED: October 8, 1869

Franklin Pierce

#14

—was one of the most popular politicians of the day and was very handsome. His looks and charm sadly did nothing to help his presidency. Pierce was bullied into getting the Kansas-Nebraska Act passed. This act would basically allow these two territories to choose whether they were for or against slavery. It would end up dividing the country further and bringing the country closer to war. This angered other states and caused powerful people (like Abraham Lincoln) to start a whole new party that opposed slavery, the Republican Party.

Tragedy seemed to follow the Pierces: Their first two sons died of disease and they would traumatically witness the death of their eleven-year-old son, Benny. His head was crushed before their eyes in a train accident. Franklin Pierce turned to alcohol to help ease the emotional pain.

Pierce was probably one of the first presidents to be arrested for drunk driving. Though it is not proven that he was drunk, it is a fact that he was driving too fast. He drove his carriage right into an old woman on the streets of Washington. He was promptly arrested and then released when they realized he was the president.

Pierce was the first president to have a full-time bodyguard at the expense of the government. This wasn't foolproof, though—someone did take aim at President Pierce with a hard-boiled egg.

Did You Know That . . .

★ Franklin Pierce's nickname was Fainting Frank due to an accident in the Mexican War?

★ Pierce was a New Hampshire senator when he was only thirty-two years old?

★ Pierce's vice president, William King, died before assuming office?

★ Pierce had no vice president his entire term?

★ While Pierce was in office, the first central-heating system was installed in the White House?

★ Franklin Pierce was a great fisherman?

★ Pierce suffered from chronic bronchitis and had a persistent cough?

★ Franklin Pierce was the first president born in the nineteenth century?

★ Franklin Pierce was five feet ten inches tall?

★ Pierce defeated his commanding officer from the Mexican War for president?

★ Pierce was the first president to give his inaugural address with no notes?

★ The Pierce administration installed plumbing in the White House?

★ Franklin Pierce was the only president not nominated by his party when he wanted to run for reelection?

★ Franklin Pierce was friends with author Nathaniel Hawthorne?

★ Jefferson Davis (future president of the Confederacy) served as Pierce's secretary of war?

★ Pierce was a very unpopular former president during the Civil War because he opposed it?

★ Pierce stopped drinking four years before his death but still died of cirrhosis of the liver?

★ Potato chips were invented during Pierce's term?

★ Franklin Pierce's father had served two terms as governor of New Hampshire and also many years in the state legislature?

★ Pierce and his wife lived on an island for two years after leaving the White House?

★ President Pierce's eyes were gray?

★ Pierce was born in a log cabin?

BIRTHDAY: April 23, 1791,
in Cove Gap, Pennsylvania

PARENTS: James and Elizabeth Speer Buchanan

FIRST LADY: None
Hostess: Harriet Lane (his niece)

KIDS: None

COLLEGE: Dickinson College

JOBS BEFORE PRESIDENT: Soldier, Lawyer,
Member of Pennsylvania House of Representatives,
Minister to Russia and England, U.S. Senator,
Secretary of State under James Polk

POLITICAL PARTY: Democratic

RELIGION: Presbyterian

AGE AT INAUGURATION: Sixty-five

YEARS IN OFFICE: 1857–1861

NICKNAME: Old Buck

DIED: June 1, 1868

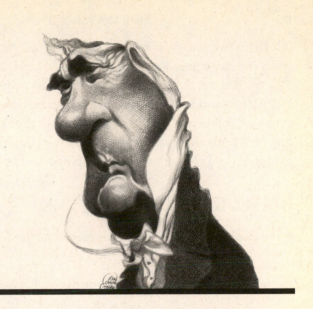

James Buchanan

#15

—was the first and only single president. During his presidency the least of his worries was his love life. He thought that slavery was supported by the Constitution but failed to do anything to compromise with those who opposed it. The nation was coming apart, and seven states seceded from the Union at the end of his presidency and formed the Confederate States of America.

His cabinet was among the most corrupt in history. They took bribes, offered kickbacks, and paid cash to those who voted their way. A relative of Buchanan's secretary of war stole over $850,000 in federal bonds. Congress did not trust anyone in the administration and turned down a plan for the United States to buy Cuba because they worried the cabinet would squander the money.

In his twenties Buchanan was engaged to Anne Coleman, who was a wealthy young woman from Pennsylvania. Her parents were concerned about the engagement and convinced her to break it off. Her parents sent her away on a trip to Philadelphia to help her forget about things and cheer her up. The trip didn't help her forget. She eventually died (some say of a broken heart). Buchanan was devastated and commented that happiness had left him forever.

Did You Know That . . .

★ James Buchanan had raised his niece Harriet Lane since she was nine?

★ Buchanan was nearsighted in one eye and farsighted in the other? (This caused him to lean his head to the left and close one eye.)

★ President Buchanan had a distinguishing feature—his left eye sat higher in its socket than his right eye?

★ James Buchanan had blue eyes?

★ Buchanan loved reading and read all the time?

★ Buchanan is known as the president with the neatest penmanship?

★ James Buchanan was the first president to receive and send a transatlantic telegram?

★ Minnesota, Oregon, and Kansas became states during Buchanan's term?

★ Buchanan had a *huge* dog, one of the biggest ever to be in the White House, named Lara? (A Newfoundland.)

★ Buchanan was known in his hometown to host sauerkraut and mashed potato parties? (Huh!)

★ Buchanan was born in a log cabin?

★ James Buchanan was the first president to have royalty stay as guests in the White House? (Once he had so many staying that he had to sleep in the hall on the floor.)

★ Buchanan was the only president to be offered elephants from a king?

★ Buchanan lived from George Washington's presidency through Abraham Lincoln's?

★ President Buchanan enjoyed alcohol, and lots of it?

★ James Buchanan had a nervous twitch that caused his head to jerk frequently?

★ President Buchanan was slightly over six feet tall?

★ Buchanan had small feet?

★ Buchanan was considered a discipline problem in school?

★ James Buchanan became a model student his senior year but was still denied the scholastic honors that he had earned due to his earlier poor behavior?

★ In retirement Buchanan supported President Lincoln and the Union?

★ Buchanan died of pneumonia and inflammation of the lining of the heart?

★ James Buchanan left an estate of $300,000?

★ Buchanan's Wheatland Estate in Lancaster, Pennsylvania, and all of his books were left to his niece Harriet Lane Johnson?

BIRTHDAY: February 12, 1809,
in Hodgenville, Kentucky

PARENTS: Thomas and Nancy Hanks Lincoln
Stepmother: Sarah Bush Johnston

FIRST LADY: Mary Todd

KIDS: Robert Todd, Edward Baker (1846–1850),
William Wallace (1850–1862),
and Thomas (Tad) Lincoln

COLLEGE: None

JOBS BEFORE PRESIDENT: Lawyer (self-taught),
Soldier, Member of Illinois State Legislature,
Congressman

POLITICAL PARTY: Republican

RELIGION: None (but read the Bible daily)

AGE AT INAUGURATION: Fifty-two

YEARS IN OFFICE: 1861–1865

NICKNAMES: Honest Abe; Illinois Rail-Splitter

DIED: April 15, 1865

Abraham Lincoln

#16

—had possibly the greatest sense of humor of any president in history. He was well known for poking fun at himself to get his points across. This quality served him well and usually caused those in his presence to perk up and listen, as well as follow him (not to mention laugh out loud). His popularity as a politician began to soar. His clever sayings were published in "books of wit and wisdom."

Abraham Lincoln was our tallest, skinniest president. He was aware of his homely appearance and often used it to make people laugh. Once, when someone disagreed with him and called him "two-faced," he commented back, "If I had two faces, do you think I would be wearing this one?" Another situation dealing with his looks involved an eleven-year-old girl who wrote him during his presidential campaign suggesting that his face was much too skinny. She said that a beard would do the trick and that ladies really liked whiskers. He took her advice and became the very first bearded U.S. president. His beard is the feature most Americans recognize him by.

Lincoln loved his kids and played with them often. Once his children broke into one of his meetings begging their father to save their pet turkey, Jack, from the looming holiday feast. He let out a hearty laugh and promised that their turkey would live. Lincoln's youngest son, Tad, loved to pretend and was given a make-believe commission as a lieutenant by Lincoln's secretary of war, Edwin Stanton. Stanton gave Tad the complete works—rank, sword, and uniform. Tad was mesmerized and taken with his new post. He promptly dismissed guards and armed the White House staff. Tad's new power went to his head—he sentenced a doll to execution. Lincoln wrote a presidential pardon to clear up the situation.

There is a huge coincidence involving Lincoln's son Robert and the assassinations of three presidents. He was invited by his parents to Ford's Theatre the night his father was shot in 1865 but did not attend. After hearing the news, he raced to his dad's bedside to be with him until he died. He had been invited to travel with President Garfield in 1881, when the president was assassinated at a Washington, D.C., train station. President McKinley invited Robert Lincoln to the Pan-American Exposition in 1901, where McKinley was speaking. President McKinley was assassinated. Robert was not an actual eyewitness to any one of the assassinations, but his presence had been requested and he had accepted (except his dad's). After President McKinley died, Robert Lincoln made it clear that he wanted no further invitations from any U.S. president ever again. His excuse? His presence had been requested at the assassinations of three U.S. presidents. It makes you wonder how his friends and family reacted when Robert Lincoln RSVP'd to a birthday party or dinner!

Did You Know That . . .

★ At six feet four inches, Lincoln was our tallest president?

★ Lincoln weighed approximately 180 pounds?

★ Lincoln was the first Republican president?

★ President Lincoln freed slaves?

★ Lincoln sometimes stowed documents and important papers in his stovepipe hat?

★ Lincoln never slept in the Lincoln Bedroom of the White House?

★ President Lincoln died five days after winning the Civil War?

★ The Lincoln Memorial was not constructed until fifty-seven years after Lincoln's death?

★ President Lincoln was one of five bearded presidents? (Lincoln, Ulysses S. Grant, Rutherford B. Hayes, James Garfield, Benjamin Harrison.)

★ Abraham Lincoln was the first president born outside the original thirteen colonies? (Kentucky.)

★ Lincoln was the only president to have had a patent? (He created a hydraulic system that raised ships over shoals.)

★ Lincoln was the first president to be killed by assassination?

★ Thirty-six states made up the United States when Lincoln was president?

★ Lincoln's was the first U.S. president's face to be on a coin—the penny?

★ The Lincoln family had many interesting pets? (A turkey named Jack, two goats named Nanny and Nanko, and a cat named Bob.)

★ Lincoln was born in a one-room cabin with dirt floors?

★ As a six-foot teenager, Abe Lincoln once lifted a chicken pen that weighed 600 pounds?

★ Lincoln went to school irregularly but was an excellent student and reader?

★ Wrestling was Lincoln's very favorite sport? (He participated as a teenager in county wrestling and no one could beat him.)

★ President Lincoln once owned a general store with a business partner?

★ Abe Lincoln became a lawyer by borrowing law books from others? (He studied for three years and passed the test.)

★ Lincoln once walked over six miles to borrow a grammar book?

★ Abe Lincoln estimated that he had a total of one year of schooling?

★ Lincoln was a very easygoing parent and loved reading to his kids?

★ *Our American Cousin* was the play that Lincoln was attending at Ford's Theatre when he was assassinated?

★ President Lincoln was killed during the second scene, third act, by John Wilkes Booth?

★ Lincoln and his wife slept in separate beds in the White House?

★ Lincoln gave his most famous speech, the Gettysburg Address, while suffering from smallpox? (He spoke to about 15,000 people.)

★ Lincoln and his wife held séances in the White House to contact their deceased sons?

★ Lincoln had a substitute in the Civil War—not a paid substitute like others, but one who volunteered in his place because he found out that Lincoln thought even the president should fight, but could not because of all the demands of his office? (His name was John Staples.)

★ Lincoln dreamed that he would be assassinated?

★ Lincoln was carried across the street from Ford's Theatre after being shot? (What is weird is that he died in the same room and bed that John Wilkes Booth had rented before.)

★ Lincoln didn't like being called Abe?

★ Lincoln's mom had died from milk poisoning when the family dairy cow ate poisonous mushrooms?

★ Lincoln established Thanksgiving as a national holiday?

★ President Lincoln loved playing marbles and did this to relieve stress during the Civil War?

★ Income tax was first used during Lincoln's administration?

★ The draft was used for the first time during Lincoln's administration to supply the army with soldiers?

★ Lincoln was the first president who received a transcontinental telegram?

★ Abe Lincoln was the first president to have a photograph taken of him at inauguration?

★ After Lincoln was killed, his body traveled to fourteen cities to lie in state?

★ There was actually a plot to steal Lincoln's body, and guards were placed at his tomb?

★ Lincoln had a wart on his right cheek and a scar over his right eye?

★ Lincoln loved the writings of Edgar Allan Poe?

★ Abraham Lincoln's oldest son, Robert, was present at the dedication of the Lincoln Memorial on May 30, 1922? (It was Robert's last public appearance.)

★ After Lincoln's death, First Lady Mary Todd Lincoln was committed to an insane asylum by her son Robert?

★ Abraham Lincoln did not like to hunt?

★ ★ ★ ★ ★ ★ ★ ★ ★ ★ ★ ★ ★ ★ ★ ★

Patriotic Stuff

- The inscription on the Liberty Bell reads: "Proclaim Liberty throughout all the land unto all the inhabitants thereof." This is from Leviticus 25:10 in the Bible.

- The Liberty Bell weighs over 2,000 pounds.

- The bell was last rung in 1846 to celebrate George Washington's birthday (it cracked and has not been rung again).

- The U.S. Capitol is where the U.S. Senate and House of Representatives meet.

- The dome on the Capitol is made of cast iron.

- The Capitol has been built, rebuilt, and restored for over two centuries.

- President Grover Cleveland accepted the Statue of Liberty on behalf of the United States. The Statue of Liberty is made of copper and is 151 feet tall. There are 354 stairs to reach the crown.

BIRTHDAY: December 29, 1808,
in Raleigh, North Carolina

PARENTS: Jacob and Mary McDonough Johnson

FIRST LADY: Eliza McCardle

KIDS: Martha, Charles, Mary, Robert,
and Andrew Johnson

COLLEGE: None

JOBS BEFORE PRESIDENT: Tailor, Mayor,
Member of Tennessee State Legislature,
Tennessee State Senator, Congressman,
Governor of Tennessee, U.S. Senator,
Vice President under Abraham Lincoln,
Military Governor of Tennessee

POLITICAL PARTY: Democratic/Unionist

RELIGION: None

AGE AT INAUGURATION: Fifty-six

YEARS IN OFFICE: 1865–1869

NICKNAMES: King Andy; Sir Veto

DIED: July 31, 1875

Andrew Johnson

#17

—was never expected to become president. He was Lincoln's choice as vice president on the ticket for his reelection bid. Lincoln wanted to have a wider appeal to Democratic voters in the border states for his second run at the presidency by having a vice presidential candidate who was a Democrat. It worked! Lincoln was elected president for a second term with Andrew Johnson as his V.P. Only five weeks into his new job, Johnson became the first vice president in history to assume office because a president had been assassinated.

Mary Todd Lincoln and Congress did not make his job any easier. Johnson had to meet with his cabinet in the U.S. Treasury building because Mrs. Lincoln took so long to vacate the White House. Congress fought Johnson at every turn. Johnson vetoed bills passed by Congress a total of twenty-nine times. Congress fought back by overturning his vetoes fifteen times. Johnson was a little full of himself and even compared himself to Jesus Christ. He once told an angry mob that God had purposely struck down Lincoln so that he could be president. Johnson's views were drastically different from Lincoln's. He granted amnesty after the Civil War to the Confederate and Southern states that had left the Union, but not freedom to the slaves. (Despite the Emancipation Proclamation, some slaves were still not free.)

Johnson remained unpopular and eventually became the first U.S. president to be impeached. If it hadn't been for one single vote in the Senate, Andrew Johnson would have been the only president to have been forcibly removed from office. Johnson is nowhere near the top of the list of greatest presidents. You do have to admit, however, that a guy who stood his ground, freed the slaves, and saved the Union was a bit of a hard act to follow.

Did You Know That . . .

★ President Johnson brought his two Jersey cows with him to the White House?

★ Andrew Johnson was intoxicated at his inauguration as vice president? (He had consumed alcohol to help ease the effects of typhoid fever.)

★ President Johnson purchased Alaska from Russia for a little over $7 million?

★ Johnson was the only president to become a U.S. senator after leaving office?

★ Andrew Johnson never spent a day in school?

★ Johnson taught himself to read and write with help from his wife?

★ Johnson had served in the Civil War?

★ Even though Johnson was a Democrat, he served as vice president to Lincoln, who was a Republican? (Would that work today?)

★ Johnson was the first of four vice presidents to assume office due to the assassination of the president?

★ President Johnson had been the only Southern senator to support the Union and not the Confederacy?

★ Johnson designed and made some of his own clothes? (He would wear only suits he had made.)

★ Johnson enjoyed attending the circus?

★ Johnson was sometimes called the Tennessee Tailor?

★ The amendment to the Constitution that officially abolished slavery was ratified during Johnson's term?

★ Johnson liked to garden?

★ Johnson believed the Constitution was more sacred than the Bible?

★ President Johnson's father had died when he was three years old? (By accident, while saving two wealthy men from drowning.)

★ Johnson was a baseball fan?

★ Nebraska became a state during Johnson's presidency?

★ President Johnson was known for feeding the mice at the White House?

★ Johnson was five feet ten inches tall?

★ President Johnson suffered from kidney stones in the White House?

★ Andrew Johnson was a great checker player?

★ Johnson was a Mason? (A club member, not a bricklayer.)

★ ★ ★ ★ ★ ★ ★ ★ ★ ★ ★ ★ ★ ★ ★ ★

Patriotic Stuff

- The Pledge of Allegiance was written in 1892 by Francis Bellamy, a Baptist minister.

- The U.S. flag has fifty stars and thirteen red and white stripes.

- The stripes represent the original thirteen colonies.

- The stars stand for each state in the Union.

- Each color on the flag has a meaning:

  White: Purity
  Red: Valor and bravery
  Blue: Perseverance and justice

BIRTHDAY: April 27, 1822,
in Point Pleasant, Ohio

PARENTS: Jesse Root and Hannah Simpson Grant

FIRST LADY: Julia Boggs Dent

KIDS: Frederick Dent, Ulysses Simpson,
Ellen Wrenshall ("Nellie"), and Jesse Root Grant

COLLEGE: U.S. Military Academy at West Point

JOBS BEFORE PRESIDENT: Soldier, Farmer,
Real Estate Agent, Interim Secretary of War
under Andrew Johnson

POLITICAL PARTY: Republican

RELIGION: Methodist

AGE AT INAUGURATION: Forty-six

YEARS IN OFFICE: 1869–1877

NICKNAMES: Useless;
Unconditional Surrender (for initials "U.S.")

DIED: July 23, 1885

Ulysses S. Grant

#18

—was one of America's first celebrities and was considered a super-star after the Civil War. He was a Civil War commander and hero and all of America knew his name. Everyone wanted him to be president, including his friends. So he ran and won by a landslide. Over 700,000 African Americans voted for Grant because he was essential to their emancipation and equality. He won without a majority of the white votes.

Grant had no political experience and ran his presidency like a military operation. He made the fatal mistake of appointing bud-dies and friends to his cabinet and other high posts, which would ultimately be his undoing. His friends were disloyal and embez-zled money from the government and others. Although Grant was not involved in this, it pretty much rested on his shoulders and presidency.

Grant died from throat cancer just weeks after finishing his memoirs. His cancer was most likely a result of his twenty-cigars-a-day habit. His memoirs were popular and sold well. His family received close to $500,000 from the book.

Grant had a "need for speed." If he were alive today, his ride of choice would most likely be the fastest sports car available and he would have several. Instead he was a master horseman and owned several horses that fed his desire to go fast. He once drag-raced former president Andrew Johnson in a carriage through Central Park in New York. He also received a ticket for speeding down M Street in Washington, D.C., on his horse.

Did You Know That . . .

★ President Grant couldn't stand the sight of blood?

★ Grant swabbed his throat each day with cocaine and became addicted to it?

★ Grant was a devoted family man and couldn't stand to be separated from his family?

★ Grant suffered from migraine headaches?

★ Ulysses Grant was drunk most of the time as a soldier?

★ Grant weighed over ten pounds at birth?

★ Ulysses Grant was five feet seven inches tall and weighed about 135 pounds during the Civil War?

★ President Grant had blue eyes?

★ Grant did not use profanity and no one around him was allowed to either?

★ Grant's first name was Hiram but he went by Ulysses?

★ Grant graduated from West Point? (One of two presidents to do so.)

★ At West Point Grant was mistakenly called Ulysses Simpson Grant and he liked it and stuck with it? (Otherwise his initials would have been H.U.G.)

★ Grant was a fourth cousin once removed to FDR?

★ President Grant loved to eat cucumbers soaked in vinegar for breakfast?

★ People sent Grant cigars because they knew he loved to smoke them, and he received over 10,000 boxes?

★ Grant didn't like music, possibly because he was tone-deaf?

★ Ulysses Grant wore false teeth?

★ Ulysses Grant received $25,000 per year as president during his first term and it was raised to $50,000 for his second term?

★ Grant loved to whittle wood?

★ Grant was the first president to run against a woman? (Victoria Woodhull.)

★ The first national park was created during Grant's administration? (Yellowstone.)

★ First Lady Julia Grant was cross-eyed?

★ The transcontinental (railroad) was completed during his administration?

★ Grant was almost court-martialed by the military for drinking so much?

★ Ulysses Grant was shy and modest and always bathed in private during his soldier days (which wasn't easy to do)?

★ Grant had his dentures accidentally thrown out during the Civil War?

★ One of Grant's favorite horses was named Jefferson Davis?

★ Grant was known to be superstitious, especially about retracing his steps?

★ Grant and his son Jesse loved to view the stars from the roof of the White House with their telescope?

★ Colorado became a state during Grant's administration?

★ The telephone was invented by Alexander Graham Bell during Grant's administration?

★ Grant had police security bar African Americans from the White House during his two terms?

★ Ulysses S. Grant was the first president to have both of his parents living when he was elected president?

★ During Grant's two terms in office he had five different men serve as attorney general?

★ President William McKinley dedicated Grant's Tomb?

★ ★ ★ ★ ★ ★ ★ ★ ★ ★ ★ ★ ★ ★ ★ ★ ★

Patriotic Stuff

- The Washington Monument is 555 feet tall and has a metal cap.

- There are four words engraved on the cap: "Praise be to God."

- Along the staircase inside the monument are Bible verses.

- The Jefferson Memorial is made solely of marble.

- In the center of the Jefferson Memorial is a nineteen-foot-high bronze statue of Thomas Jefferson.

BIRTHDAY: October 4, 1822, in Delaware, Ohio

PARENTS: Rutherford and Sophia Birchard Hayes

FIRST LADY: Lucy Ware Webb

KIDS: Sardis Birchard Austin, James Webb Cook, Rutherford Platt, Joseph Thompson (1861–1863), George Crook (1864–1866), Frances ("Fanny"), Scott Russell, and Manning Force (1873–1874) Hayes

COLLEGES: Kenyon College; Harvard Law School

JOBS BEFORE PRESIDENT: Lawyer, Soldier, Congressman, Governor of Ohio

POLITICAL PARTY: Republican

RELIGION: Methodist

AGE AT INAUGURATION: Fifty-four

YEARS IN OFFICE: 1877–1881

NICKNAMES: Rutherfraud Hayes; His Fraudulency

DIED: January 17, 1893

Rutherford B. Hayes

#19

—was probably one of the most religious U.S. presidents in history. His wife, Lucy Hayes, was given the nickname Lemonade Lucy because she refused to serve any type of alcohol (wine and beer included) in the White House and would offer lemonade instead. Each night at the White House the Hayes family could be found singing gospel songs and hymns. On many occasions the family would be joined by members of the cabinet, who helped sing and play piano. Each and every morning the Hayes family would begin the day on their knees in prayer. During this administration Mrs. Hayes made sure there would be no funny business. She banned all card playing, dancing, and smoking from any event held at the White House. She also got rid of the pool table that Ulysses Grant had moved into the Executive Mansion.

The Hayes election was the most disputed in history. Yes, even more than the election of 2000. Hayes lost the popular vote and results were disputed in three states—South Carolina, Louisiana, and, you guessed it, Florida (when will these people learn?!). Each state had recounts and ended up with two completely different accounts of the electoral vote. There was a committee appointed by Congress to sift through the results. There were no hanging-chad counters but rather a committee of eight Republicans and seven Democrats, who ended their investigation right along party lines. Hayes became president. The election earned him the unwanted nicknames of Rutherfraud Hayes and His Fraudulency. Anger and emotion prevailed over the results, but Hayes promised to run an administration of integrity and to reach across party lines (doesn't everyone promise this?). He also vowed to serve only one term and did (no one promises this anymore!).

When the Hayes family was not busy praying, singing hymns, or drinking lemonade, they could be found sitting around waiting for their phone to ring. The only requirement for calling them was to have a phone yourself and to remember their phone number, which was as easy as 1-2-3 . . . well, not even 1-2-3 but just 1. Yes, just 1—that was their phone number. I wonder whose number was 2? How about 3?

Did You Know That . . .

★ Hayes had the first telephone installed in the White House?

★ Hayes's first phone conversation was with Alexander Graham Bell, thirteen miles away?

★ Hayes was one of seven presidents to serve in the Civil War? (He was a general.)

★ Rutherford Hayes was the only president to have been wounded in the Civil War?

★ Hayes had an easygoing personality?

★ President Hayes dressed simply in slouchy clothes?

★ Hayes was the first president to take the oath of office in the White House?

★ Rutherford Hayes was the first president to visit the West Coast?

★ Lucy hosted the very first Easter Egg Roll on the White House lawn? (The tradition had started at the Capitol.)

★ Lucy Hayes was the first presidential wife referred to as First Lady of the Land?

★ Lucy Hayes was the first First Lady to have a college degree?

★ Hayes's father had died before he was born?

★ Hayes removed several people from government office who he felt were corrupt and using their positions to further their own causes? (This included Chester A. Arthur, a future president.)

★ Hayes was very close to his sister? (She died giving birth to twins in 1856 and he was devastated.)

★ Hayes's Republican Party was trying to stamp out polygamy?

★ Hayes's son Webb was his personal secretary?

★ Hayes was the first president to graduate from law school?

★ The lightbulb was invented during the Hayes administration?

★ Lucy Hayes loved pets and had three birds, four cats, five dogs, a goat, and a peacock in the White House? (She referred to this as her "Noah collection.")

★ The Hayes family owned the first Siamese cat in America?

★ The Hayes family was the wealthiest to live in the White House up to the Hayes presidency?

★ Rutherford Hayes was five feet eight and a half inches tall and weighed around 180 pounds?

★ President Hayes recalled believing as a child that he had a great power inside him?

★ Rutherford Hayes was involved in a serious train wreck when he retired? (He was unhurt.)

★ Hayes died after having a heart attack? (He was with his son Webb.)

★ ★ ★ ★ ★ ★ ★ ★ ★ ★ ★ ★ ★ ★ ★ ★

Presidents Who Served in Wars

GEORGE WASHINGTON: Commander in Chief, Continental Army—American Revolution

JAMES MONROE: American Revolution

ANDREW JACKSON: American Revolution, First Seminole War, War of 1812

WILLIAM HENRY HARRISON: Indian Wars in Northwest Territory, War of 1812

JOHN TYLER: War of 1812

ZACHARY TAYLOR: War of 1812, Black Hawk War, Second Seminole War, Mexican War

FRANKLIN PIERCE: Mexican War

JAMES BUCHANAN: War of 1812

ABRAHAM LINCOLN: Black Hawk War

ANDREW JOHNSON: Civil War

ULYSSES S. GRANT: Mexican War, Civil War

RUTHERFORD B. HAYES: Civil War

(continued on page 113)

BIRTHDAY: November 19, 1831,
in Orange Township, Ohio

PARENTS: Abram and Eliza Ballou Garfield

FIRST LADY: Lucretia Rudolph

KIDS: Eliza Arabella (1860–1863), Harry Augustus,
James Rudolph, Mary ("Molly"), Irvin McDowell,
Abram, and Edward Abram (1874–1876) Garfield

COLLEGE: Williams College

JOBS BEFORE PRESIDENT: Teacher, Soldier,
Ohio State Senator, Congressman

POLITICAL PARTY: Republican

RELIGION: Disciples of Christ

AGE AT INAUGURATION: Forty-nine

YEAR IN OFFICE: 1881

NICKNAMES: Preacher President;
the Teacher President

DIED: September 19, 1881

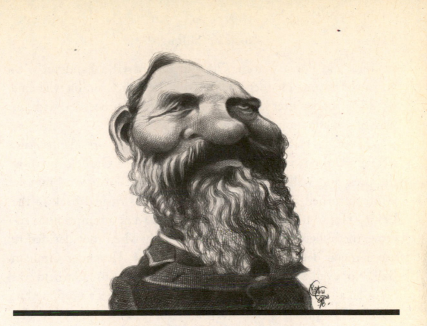

James Garfield

#20

—had packed his bags and was on his way out of Washington. His wife had contracted malaria from the swamps behind the White House and the president had sent her to New Jersey to recuperate and regain her strength. An insane man named Charles Guiteau would change not only their plans but their lives and U.S. history.

Guiteau had supported Garfield during his campaign for president and expected a government position for his efforts. He had his own plan to someday be the president. He would appear daily at the White House requesting to see the president and to speak with him about opportunities. His ideal job was to be minister to either Austria or France. He began to be a nuisance to the White House staff. Garfield's staff told him all jobs were filled. He soon began stalking the president and was asked to leave the grounds and not to return. Guiteau purchased a handgun with borrowed money. He then checked out the police station where he would surrender after killing the president and proceeded with his plan of assassination.

There was no Secret Service in those days and presidents didn't wear bulletproof vests. Guiteau shot President Garfield twice as the president walked through a railroad station in Washington. Guiteau turned himself in and Garfield was rushed back to the White House to be treated. The doctors were attempting to remove the bullets from the president's body when they decided to use a metal detector, the new invention of Alexander Graham Bell. Not even this device could assist them because Garfield was lying on a bed of springs and it was unable to detect anything but springs. The president was moved by train to New Jersey so that his family could care for him in private and he could escape the heat of Washington in July. From Washington to New Jersey, straw had been scattered over the railroad tracks in order to make the trip smoother and more comfortable for the president. Because of all the probing of the doctors, their unsterile hands and instruments, Garfield eventually died of blood poisoning.

Did You Know That . . .

★ President Garfield could write Greek with one hand and Latin with the other?

★ James Garfield worked as a kid on a canal boat and fell overboard fourteen times?

★ Garfield did not know how to swim?

★ President Garfield had experienced long bouts of depression?

★ Garfield was one of six presidents to be born in a log cabin?

★ James Garfield was the only man in history who was a U.S. congressman, senator-elect, and president-elect all at the same time?

★ Garfield campaigned for the presidency by giving speeches from the front porch of his house?

★ James Garfield was the first president to watch the inauguration parade from in front of the White House?

★ Garfield campaigned in more than one language? (English and German.)

★ Robert Todd, Abraham Lincoln's son, was Garfield's secretary of war?

★ Garfield was the very first left-handed president?

★ The Garfields' dog was named Veto?

★ Garfield was one of four presidents to be assassinated?

★ James Garfield was a great juggler and did this for fitness reasons?

★ Garfield was the only president to have been a preacher?

★ Lucretia Garfield was the first First Lady to take inventory of the things in the White House?

★ First Lady Lucretia Garfield spent lots of time in the Library of Congress researching the history of the White House and its contents?

★ Garfield supposedly talked to Robert Todd Lincoln about every detail of his father's assassination?

★ President Garfield took out a life insurance policy of $25,000 shortly before he died?

★ Public donations of over $300,000 poured in for the Garfield family after the president's assassination?

★ President Garfield had an extramarital affair?

★ When Garfield was nominated for president at the 1880 Republican Convention, he received no votes on the first ballot?

★ President Garfield was on his deathbed for eighty days?

★ Garfield had led a fairly sheltered life—he was nineteen before he heard piano music for the first time and twenty-three before he had tasted a banana?

★ Garfield came from the poorest background of any president?

★ Garfield was said to have been three years old when he learned to read?

★ Garfield had nightmares regularly?

★ James Garfield was six feet tall and weighed about 185 pounds?

★ President Garfield had light brown hair and blue eyes?

★ Garfield walked at nine months old?

★ Garfield loved reading American history and sea adventures as a youth?

★ ★ ★ ★ ★ ★ ★ ★ ★ ★ ★ ★ ★ ★ ★ ★

Presidents Who Served in Wars

(continued)

JAMES GARFIELD: Civil War

CHESTER ARTHUR: Civil War

BENJAMIN HARRISON: Civil War

WILLIAM MCKINLEY: Civil War

THEODORE ROOSEVELT: Spanish-American War

HARRY TRUMAN: World War I

DWIGHT EISENHOWER: World War I, World War II

JOHN F. KENNEDY: World War II

LYNDON B. JOHNSON: World War II

RICHARD NIXON: World War II

GERALD FORD: World War II

GEORGE H. W. BUSH: World War II

BIRTHDAY: October 5, 1829,
in Fairfield, Vermont

PARENTS: William and Malvina Stone Arthur

FIRST LADY: None

HOSTESS: Mary Arthur McElroy (his sister)

KIDS: William Lewis Herndon (1860–1863),
Chester Alan, and Ellen Herndon Arthur

COLLEGE: Union College

JOBS BEFORE PRESIDENT: Teacher, Lawyer,
Soldier, Vice President under James Garfield

POLITICAL PARTY: Republican

RELIGION: Episcopalian

AGE AT INAUGURATION: Fifty-one

YEARS IN OFFICE: 1881–1885

NICKNAMES: Elegant Arthur; the Gentleman Boss

DIED: November 18, 1886

Chester Alan Arthur

#21

—was known for his New York style and class. He loved fine wine, elegant clothes (and lots of them), and fancy Victorian furnishings. When Arthur was elected vice president, he was said to have celebrated at (ready for this?) *Brooks Brothers*. He purchased a closetful of clothes as a reward to himself. President Arthur owned over eighty pairs of pants and changed them several times a day. He was always an immaculate dresser with impeccable taste. Arthur was the first president to have a personal valet, and he wore a full set of sideburns that distinguished him even more.

His taste was so exquisite that when he became president he refused to move into the White House. He declared it a dump and had twenty-four wagonloads of furniture and junk removed from the executive premises. Arthur held an auction and sold all of the removed furniture and used the proceeds to refurbish and remodel his new crib. He wanted the job done right, so he hired New York designer Louis Tiffany to redecorate. Tiffany and Arthur collaborated on a formal Victorian style. To complete his formal surroundings he hired a full-time French chef to accommodate his culinary desires.

Arthur was very devoted to his wife, Ellen Lewis Herndon Arthur, who died before he was president. He had a stained-glass window built in his church in her memory. Each day the White House staff placed fresh flowers next to her picture.

After entertaining his guests over gourmet dinners, Arthur was known to stroll, with his guests or sometimes alone, through the streets of Washington until 3 or 4 A.M. With these hours it was a good thing that President Arthur took a power nap each day and didn't arrive in the office until 10 A.M. He usually never worked past 4 P.M., and put off anything that could wait until tomorrow. What a life!

Did You Know That . . .

★ President Arthur played the banjo?

★ New York City was lit by electricity during Arthur's administration?

★ The Brooklyn Bridge was completed in 1883, during Arthur's administration?

★ Arthur was considered very emotional and cried easily?

★ Arthur was the first president to have Bright's disease? (Kidney disease.)

★ Arthur's reputation of being a corrupt New York politician changed as he ran a completely honest administration in the White House?

★ Chester Arthur's birthplace is not really known? (Some say he was born in Vermont and others say he was born in New York in a log cabin. There were others who alleged that he was actually born across the Vermont border in Canada, and this became an issue during the campaign with Garfield. Most believed Vermont to be his birthplace.)

★ Chester Arthur's wife had supported the Confederacy during the Civil War?

★ The only office Arthur was ever elected to was the office of vice president?

★ Chester Arthur was named after the doctor who delivered him?

★ Arthur never let his kids be interviewed or photographed while he was president?

★ President Arthur was a very respected fisherman of his day?

★ Arthur once caught an eighty-pound bass?

★ President Arthur was responsible for the first immigration laws?

★ When Arthur left the White House, he was going to retire and raise big pumpkins?

★ President Arthur died of Bright's disease at age fifty-six, about a year after leaving the White House?

★ Arthur was six feet two inches tall?

★ President Arthur weighed about 225 pounds?

★ Chester Arthur's dad was a preacher?

★ President Arthur was a prankster in college?

★ ★ ★ ★ ★ ★ ★ ★ ★ ★ ★ ★ ★ ★ ★

Presidents Who Served in the Military but Never in a War

JAMES MADISON

JAMES POLK

MILLARD FILLMORE

JIMMY CARTER

RONALD REAGAN
(not in combat due to poor eyesight)

GEORGE W. BUSH

BIRTHDAY: March 18, 1837,
in Caldwell, New Jersey

PARENTS: Richard and Anne Neal Cleveland

FIRST LADY: Frances Folsom

KIDS: Ruth, Esther, Marion, Richard Folsom,
and Francis Grover Cleveland

COLLEGE: None

JOBS BEFORE PRESIDENT: Lawyer, Sheriff,
Mayor, Governor of New York

POLITICAL PARTY: Democratic

RELIGION: Presbyterian

AGE AT INAUGURATION: Forty-seven

YEARS IN OFFICE: 1885–1889 and 1893–1897

NICKNAMES: Uncle Jumbo; Buffalo Hangman;
His Obstinacy

DIED: June 24, 1908

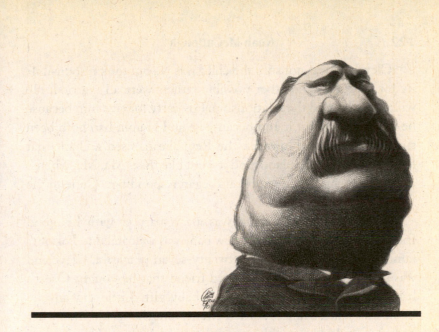

Grover Cleveland
#22 and #24

—was known as one of the most honest presidents. Really? Listen to this: The campaign of 1884 was one of the dirtiest on record. As Grover Cleveland ran for the highest job in the land, it was discovered that he once had an affair with a woman whose main job was having lots of affairs, but usually with married men. Her name was Maria Halpin and she had her sights set on bachelor Grover Cleveland. When she discovered that she was going to have a baby, she insisted that Cleveland was the father. The Republicans found out and plastered the papers with the news. When asked by his panicked staff how they should respond to this, Cleveland answered, "Just tell them the truth!" What a concept: an honest immoral person.

Cleveland was not sure the child was his but took responsibility for it because the other possible fathers were all married. He willingly admitted the relationship. His party forgave him because he was honest about it and because he and Halpin had both been single at the time. However, the Republicans used a chant that haunted Grover Cleveland, and it went like this: "Ma, Ma, where's my pa?" To which the Democrats began responding: "Gone to the White House, ha, ha, ha."

As a bachelor, Cleveland was a law partner with his good friend Oscar Folsom. When a new baby was welcomed to Folsom's family, Grover Cleveland was twenty-seven years old. Cleveland was so excited and such a devoted friend that he bought Oscar's baby, Frances, a new carriage as a baby gift. Little did anyone know that when Frances turned twenty-one, he would marry her and she would become the youngest First Lady in U.S. history. They were also the only First Couple to marry in the actual White House.

Grover Cleveland had a secret surgery during his presidency that was not discovered until almost twenty-five years later. He wanted this so secret that the surgery was performed on the yacht of one of his friends. The yacht sailed to Long Island Sound for the procedure. Cleveland's personal physician performed the operation. The president had a cancerous growth on the roof of his mouth and a lot of his jaw had to be removed. It was replaced with a prosthetic rubber jaw.

Grover Cleveland was the twenty-second and twenty-fourth president of the United States. He was the only president to serve two nonconsecutive terms. Cleveland lost reelection to Benjamin Harrison after his first term. He and his wife told the White House staff, "Take good care of the place. *We'll be back!*" Hey . . . didn't someone else say that? (Hint: governor of California.)

Did You Know That . . .

★ On his wedding day President Cleveland worked right up until the 7 P.M. ceremony?

★ At 250 pounds Cleveland was one of our heaviest presidents? (Not *the* heaviest, though.)

★ Grover Cleveland was said to have had a bit of a dual personality? (He was happy and then quick-tempered.)

★ Cleveland was the first Democratic president elected after the Civil War?

★ Grover Cleveland was the first president to have a child born in the White House? (His daughter Esther.)

★ The Baby Ruth candy bar was named after Cleveland's baby daughter Ruth?

★ President Cleveland and the First Lady shook over 8,000 hands at the White House New Year's Day reception?

★ Cleveland answered the telephone in the White House personally? (Cool!)

★ President Cleveland named his favorite hunting rifle "Death and Destruction"?

★ Cleveland had been a draft dodger? (He hired someone to serve in his place—it was legal to do so back then.)

★ Grover Cleveland was the first and only president to be born in New Jersey?

★ Cleveland was the first president to use fireworks at his inauguration?

★ Cleveland was the first president since the Civil War not to have served in it?

★ Grover Cleveland was distantly related to Ulysses S. Grant?

★ The Cleveland family had pet mockingbirds, canaries, and a dog?

★ During his first term Cleveland was at his desk until two or three in the morning working?

★ Within a span of almost four years Cleveland had been the mayor of Buffalo, New York; the governor of New York State; and the president of the United States?

★ Cleveland had been a sheriff and actually had to pull the hangman lever to hang individuals for their crimes?

★ President Cleveland vetoed more than 300 bills during his first term?

★ President Cleveland called his wife, Frances, "Frank"?

★ John Philip Sousa's band provided wedding music for the Clevelands' wedding?

★ Cleveland loved beer and cigars?

★ Grover Cleveland attributed his political success to his mom's prayers for him?

★ Cleveland enjoyed German food?

★ President Cleveland loved to fish and hunt?

★ On Sundays Grover Cleveland played poker instead of going to church?

★ Cleveland and his wife, Frances, sent out pieces of their leftover wedding cake as gifts?

★ The Clevelands often retreated to Red Top, his personal getaway estate outside the city of Washington, D.C., during his presidency?

★ Grover Cleveland is on the $1,000 bill?

★ Utah became a state during Cleveland's administration?

★ The first Coca-Cola was produced during Cleveland's presidency?

★ During Cleveland's second term Cracker Jack was invented? (Yum!)

★ President Cleveland was five feet eleven inches tall?

★ Cleveland had brown hair and blue eyes?

★ When Cleveland retired, he wrote articles for the *Saturday Evening Post*?

★ Cleveland died of heart failure?

BIRTHDAY: August 20, 1833,
in North Bend, Ohio

PARENTS: John Scott and
Elizabeth Ramsey Irwin Harrison

FIRST LADY: Caroline Lavinia Scott

KIDS: Russell Benjamin, Mary Scott,
Baby (died at birth), and Elizabeth Harrison

COLLEGE: Miami (Ohio) University

JOBS BEFORE PRESIDENT: Lawyer, Soldier,
U.S. Senator

POLITICAL PARTY: Republican

RELIGION: Presbyterian

AGE AT INAUGURATION: Fifty-five

YEARS IN OFFICE: 1889–1893

NICKNAMES: The White House Iceberg; Little Ben;
the Centennial President

DIED: March 13, 1901

Benjamin Harrison

#23

—was the first and only president to be the grandson of a former president. That's right, Benjamin Harrison was the grandson of William Henry Harrison (he would have been so proud). What is really cool is that Benjamin Harrison's father, John Scott Harrison, was both the son and father of a president.

When Benjamin Harrison became president, eleven other members of his family moved into the White House with him and his wife. There was only one problem with this scenario: The White House at that time had only one bathroom . . . huh!

During Harrison's presidency the White House was modernized with electricity. The president and his wife were so scared to touch the switches that the lights in the White House stayed on all night long.

Harrison had one of the most colorful White House pets of any president. This was his goat, named His Whiskers. This billy goat was a gift to his grandchildren. Sometimes the stable workers would hook the goat to a cart and Harrison's grandchildren would take a ride. One day His Whiskers was feeling his oats when the grandchildren stepped aboard. He took off running and it was evident that he wasn't coming back. The president himself ran after the goat, chasing him up and down the streets of Washington. What a sight that must have been!

Did You Know That . . .

★ First Lady Caroline Harrison officially started the White House china collection? (She found china stored in the White House that had been used in other administrations.)

★ Harrison wore a full thick beard and mustache?

★ The first Christmas tree in the White House was in the second-floor Yellow Oval Room (then used as a family parlor and library) in 1889, during Harrison's administration?

★ Harrison was one of just three presidents to try a case before the Supreme Court after leaving office? (The other two were John Quincy Adams and Grover Cleveland.)

★ Harrison had an outstanding legal career? (His career was known as one of the best in U.S. history. When his presidency was over, he picked up right where he had left off.)

★ North Dakota, South Dakota, Wyoming, Montana, Washington, and Idaho were admitted to the Union during his term?

★ Harrison wore kid gloves (goatskin) to protect his hands from skin-infection problems that he suffered? (He was sometimes called Kid Gloves.)

★ Harrison was one of seven presidents from Ohio?

★ Harrison lost the popular vote but won the electoral?

★ Harrison was sometimes referred to as the Centennial President? (He was inaugurated 100 years after George Washington.)

★ Benjamin Harrison was the second president whose wife died in office?

★ Harrison was the last president to wear a beard?

★ President Harrison stood five feet six inches tall?

★ Harrison was the first president to be born in another president's home? (His grandfather William Henry Harrison's.)

★ Harrison created a cool campaign device called "the campaign ball," which they rolled from Maryland to Indianapolis? (It had a forty-two-inch circumference and weighed 1,000 pounds!)

★ Harrison was the first president to fly the U.S. flag from the White House and other public buildings?

★ Benjamin Harrison remarried four years after his wife's death? (He married the woman who had been his sick wife's nurse. He had a daughter with his new wife who was younger than his grandchildren.)

★ President Harrison appointed a former slave named Frederick Douglass as the ambassador to Haiti?

★ Harrison would be the last Civil War general to serve as president?

★ Benjamin Harrison spent very little time in the office? (He was gone most days by lunchtime.)

★ Harrison hired someone to catch all the rats in the White House when he moved in?

★ President Harrison once made 140 speeches in one month? (He was on a political tour and never used a speech more than once.)

★ Harrison had blue eyes?

★ President Harrison enjoyed duck hunting?

★ Harrison liked to play pool?

★ ★ ★ ★ ★ ★ ★ ★ ★ ★ ★ ★ ★ ★ ★ ★

Presidents with
No Military Experience

JOHN ADAMS

THOMAS JEFFERSON

JOHN QUINCY ADAMS

MARTIN VAN BUREN

GROVER CLEVELAND

WILLIAM TAFT

WOODROW WILSON

WARREN HARDING

CALVIN COOLIDGE

HERBERT HOOVER

FRANKLIN D. ROOSEVELT

BILL CLINTON

BIRTHDAY: January 29, 1843, in Niles, Ohio

PARENTS: William and
Nancy Campbell Allison McKinley

FIRST LADY: Ida Saxton

KIDS: Katherine (1871–1875)
and Ida (1873) McKinley

COLLEGE: Allegheny College

JOBS BEFORE PRESIDENT: Soldier, Lawyer,
Congressman, Governor of Ohio

POLITICAL PARTY: Republican

RELIGION: Methodist

AGE AT INAUGURATION: Fifty-four

YEARS IN OFFICE: 1897–1901

NICKNAMES: Wobbly Willie; Idol of Ohio

DIED: September 14, 1901

William McKinley

#25

—would watch the United States become a real world power during his presidency. The United States gained control of Guam, Puerto Rico, the Philippines, Cuba, and Hawaii. President McKinley was very corporate minded and this helped America to expand and gain wealth and power. His management of press issues was ahead of his time and close to what is common today (i.e., press releases, press conferences). He was a very popular and beloved president.

In his lapel President McKinley almost always wore a red carnation, which he considered a good-luck charm. He would often mingle in crowds after he spoke and give his carnation as a gesture of kindness or fondness. Right after his second inauguration he had just finished speaking in Buffalo, New York, at the Pan-American

Exposition. He was shaking hands and greeting his public when he gave his carnation to a shy young girl. Minutes after handing her his lucky carnation, a mentally deranged man approached the president with a fake bandaged hand. Under the bandage was a gun, and as the president reached out to shake his hand, the man fired two shots, fatally injuring McKinley. The assassin's name was Leon Czolgosz. As the president fell, the police and others began jumping on Czolgosz, beating and punching him. President McKinley yelled out, "Don't hurt him!" McKinley died eight days after the shooting from infection of the gunshot wounds.

First Lady Ida McKinley hated the color yellow. She had everything yellow removed from the White House and even made sure all of the yellow roses were dug up from the White House grounds. She suffered from epilepsy and often had seizures. The president was very protective of her. She was not an active First Lady but did perform many duties when she was feeling well. She spent lots of time in her rocking chair crocheting. She once crocheted over 3,500 pairs of slippers and donated them to charity. The president would often buck tradition by having the First Lady seated right next to him at formal events. He did this so that when she had a seizure, he could throw his napkin over her head so that she would not be embarrassed. Which is more embarrassing, suffering a seizure or your husband throwing a napkin over your head?

Did You Know That . . .

★ McKinley was well groomed and even tempered?

★ Because of the untimely deaths of her children, McKinley's wife was devastated and suffered many health problems for the rest of her life?

★ McKinley was technically the first president to ride in an automobile? (He rode in an electric ambulance to the hospital when he was shot.)

★ William McKinley was the first president to campaign by telephone?

★ McKinley's commanding officer in the Civil War was Rutherford B. Hayes?

★ McKinley was the only clean-shaven president between Andrew Johnson and Woodrow Wilson?

★ President McKinley had a pet parrot at the White House that could whistle "Yankee Doodle"?

★ The parrot and McKinley performed duets where he would whistle the first part and the parrot would whistle the second part?

★ McKinley refused to be photographed unless he was dressed in formal attire?

★ As a young boy, McKinley almost drowned?

★ McKinley loved plays by William Shakespeare?

★ Pepsi was invented during McKinley's term?

★ The very first U.S. subway system opened in Boston during McKinley's administration?

★ McKinley was the last president to have served in the Civil War?

★ McKinley was the first president to have his inauguration filmed?

★ McKinley had a habit of not only smoking cigars but also biting them and chewing them?

★ McKinley loved to smoke cigars but refused to ever be photographed with one? (He didn't want to be a bad example.)

★ When McKinley was eligible to vote, his first presidential vote was for Abraham Lincoln?

★ William McKinley established the first presidential press conferences?

★ McKinley was the first president to use campaign buttons?

★ The McKinleys once served a seventy-one-course meal at one of the White House dinners they hosted?

★ There was an elevator in the White House when McKinley was president? (It was operated by water pressure. Many times the pressure was too low to operate it.)

★ Because McKinley's mom was very ill when he became president, he had a special telegraph line between the White House and his mom's home in Canton, Ohio, installed?

★ President McKinley once received a seventy-eight-pound watermelon that was wrapped in a flag from people in Georgia who liked him?

★ McKinley was five feet seven inches tall and weighed almost 200 pounds?

★ As a kid, McKinley enjoyed fishing, camping, ice-skating, horseback riding, and swimming?

★ McKinley didn't exercise very much?

★ At his inauguration, McKinley kissed the Bible, opened it, and quoted 2 Chronicles 1:10?

★ President McKinley loved to sing hymns and invited guests over to join him?

BIRTHDAY: October 27, 1858,
in New York, New York

PARENTS: Theodore and Martha Bulloch Roosevelt

FIRST LADIES: Alice Hathaway Lee and
Edith Kermit Carow

KIDS: Alice Lee, Theodore, Kermit, Ethel Carow,
Archibald Bulloch, and Quentin Roosevelt

COLLEGE: Harvard

JOBS BEFORE PRESIDENT: Member of New York
State Assembly, Rancher, Author, New York City
Police Commissioner, Soldier, Governor of
New York, Assistant Secretary of the Navy
and Vice President under William McKinley

POLITICAL PARTY: Republican

RELIGION: Dutch Reformed

AGE AT INAUGURATION: Forty-two

YEARS IN OFFICE: 1901–1909

NICKNAMES: TR; Hero of San Juan Hill;
the Bull Moose

DIED: January 6, 1919

Theodore Roosevelt
#26

—was the most exciting, youthful, energetic, and vocal president that the United States had ever known. He was extremely confident and decisive. Roosevelt had been president for only three years when he acted on his mission to build the Panama Canal. After years of Roosevelt negotiating and even threatening to go to war with Colombia, the Panama Canal became a reality. This passageway saved U.S. and other foreign merchant ships as well as the U.S. Navy countless hours at sea. Historians have written that the Panama Canal would never have been built if it weren't for President Roosevelt.

TR helped a developing world power (the United States) become a top world power of the twentieth century. With the canal, new territories gained by McKinley, and economic growth, America was on its way to becoming the most powerful nation.

Many national parks and forests are in existence today because of Theodore Roosevelt. We can thank him for the first regulations that set safe standards for America's food and water.

Teddy Roosevelt was as tough as nails, yet when it came to children and animals, his "Rough Rider" personality turned into that of a teddy bear. Once, on a safari with his son Kermit, Roosevelt refused to shoot a baby bear cub. When toy makers of the day got wind of this, they paid tribute to the cub and President Roosevelt by presenting a new toy known affectionately as the "Teddy bear."

Roosevelt proclaimed one hour of each day as "children's hour." During this hour he would play and talk with all six of his kids. He wrestled, chased, tickled, and conducted White House pillow fights that were hard to stop. He loved his children deeply and tried to spend quality time with each of them. They were energetic and active just like their father and sometimes he would have to redirect their actions. His sons were known for pelting the portrait of Andrew Jackson with spitballs as well as dropping water balloons from the roof of the White House onto the guards below. His daughters would slide down the stairs of the White House on cookie sheets from the kitchen. They also liked to bring out their pet king snake among White House visitors just for effect. The Roosevelt children made sure the Executive Mansion was never a dull place.

Did You Know That . . .

★ Teddy Roosevelt was five feet eight inches tall?

★ Roosevelt was a cowboy?

★ Roosevelt was blind in his left eye from a boxing match?

★ Roosevelt's children named their many pets after real people? These included

- a black bear cub named Jonathan Edwards
- a badger named Josiah
- dogs named Jack and Skip
- a blue macaw named Eli
- ponies called Algonquin and General Grant
- a kitten named Tom Quartz
- a pet garden snake called Emily Spinach
- a hamster and guinea pig called Bishop and Doane

★ Roosevelt drank a gallon of coffee each day?

★ Teddy Roosevelt had a heart condition from college age through the rest of his life?

★ Roosevelt ate game that he hunted and killed on his expeditions, and he also liked beef, potatoes, and asparagus?

★ Roosevelt was a Spanish-American War hero?

★ Roosevelt was the first president to ride in an airplane? (In 1910, after he left office.)

★ Teddy Roosevelt was also the first president to be submerged in a submarine?

★ Roosevelt was the first president to own his own automobile and have a telephone in his home?

★ Roosevelt was the first American and first president to win a Nobel Peace Prize (and over $36,000), which he won for his efforts in ending the Russo-Japanese War?

★ President Roosevelt tried and failed to get "In God We Trust" removed from coins? (He thought it was unconstitutional.)

★ Roosevelt suffered from asthma as a child?

★ President Roosevelt loved to be the center of attention?

★ President Roosevelt did not smoke and rarely drank?

★ Roosevelt had an extra pair of eyeglasses sewn to his clothes during the Spanish-American War?

★ Teddy Roosevelt's mother and his first wife died on the very same day, Valentine's Day, 1884?

★ Roosevelt never spoke of his first wife, Alice, again, not even in his own autobiography?

★ When his mom and first wife, Alice, died, TR dealt with his devastation by spending two years as a cattle rancher in the Dakota Territory?

★ Theodore Roosevelt and his friends organized a military group known as the Rough Riders?

★ Roosevelt wore a bushy mustache?

★ Roosevelt taught Sunday school at an Episcopal church while he was a Harvard student?

★ Teddy Roosevelt was the first president to have his voice recorded?

★ Roosevelt's favorite hobbies were hunting, fishing, martial arts, tennis, and nude swims in the Potomac?

★ Roosevelt used to jog around the Washington Monument?

★ The Wright brothers flew the first airplane at Kitty Hawk during Roosevelt's administration?

★ First Lady Edith Roosevelt created the First Lady portrait gallery?

★ Edith Roosevelt and Teddy Roosevelt were playmates as children?

★ Ice cream cones made their debut during TR's administration?

★ Oklahoma became a state during Roosevelt's presidency?

★ Roosevelt was known to read two or three books a day?

★ President Roosevelt wrote thirty books?

★ Roosevelt actually became the first president to use the term "White House" on stationery?

★ Teddy Roosevelt was Eleanor Roosevelt's uncle and also the fifth cousin of Franklin Delano Roosevelt?

★ Everyone in the Roosevelt family owned his own pair of stilts? (Cool!)

★ Roosevelt tried to laugh at least 100 times per day?

★ Teddy Roosevelt was awarded the Congressional Medal of Honor?

★ Roosevelt's children took their pony Algonquin on the elevator of the White House to visit their brother who wasn't feeling well?

★ President Roosevelt weighed around 200 pounds?

★ Roosevelt took boxing lessons as a kid because he kept getting beat up?

★ President Roosevelt appointed Oliver Wendell Holmes to the Supreme Court?

★ Roosevelt was shot when he campaigned against William Howard Taft on the Bull Moose ticket?

★ The bullet passed through his campaign speech in his pocket as well as his eyeglass case and into his chest? (He gave the speech before going to the hospital.)

★ Roosevelt died of a coronary embolism?

★ Theodore Roosevelt left his $500,000 estate to his wife and a $60,000 trust fund to be divided among his children?

★ ★ ★ ★ ★ ★ ★ ★ ★ ★ ★ ★ ★ ★ ★

There Have Been . . .
Fourteen Democratic Presidents:

ANDREW JACKSON

MARTIN VAN BUREN

JAMES POLK

FRANKLIN PIERCE

JAMES BUCHANAN

ANDREW JOHNSON

GROVER CLEVELAND

WOODROW WILSON

FRANKLIN D. ROOSEVELT

HARRY TRUMAN

JOHN F. KENNEDY

LYNDON B. JOHNSON

JIMMY CARTER

BILL CLINTON

BIRTHDAY: September 15, 1857,
in Cincinnati, Ohio

PARENTS: Alphonso and Louisa Maria Torrey Taft

FIRST LADY: Helen ("Nellie") Herron

KIDS: Robert Alphonso, Helen Herron,
and Charles Phelps Taft

COLLEGES: Yale; Cincinnati Law School

JOBS BEFORE PRESIDENT: Lawyer, Law Professor,
Judge, U.S. Solicitor General, Governor of
the Philippines, Secretary of War
under Theodore Roosevelt

POLITICAL PARTY: Republican

RELIGION: Unitarian

AGE AT INAUGURATION: Fifty-one

YEARS IN OFFICE: 1909–1913

NICKNAME: Big Bill

DIED: March 8, 1930

William Howard Taft

#27

—was one of the few presidents who never really wanted to be president. He was not a politician at heart and had no desire to be the chief executive. His former boss Teddy Roosevelt encouraged him to run, but the real reason he ran for the job of president of the United States was to please his wife, Nellie. No joke! Her main goal in life was to be the First Lady and live in the White House.

What Taft desired more than anything was to be the chief justice of the Supreme Court, but that would have to wait until nine years after he left the White House. In his chief justice role, he would do something no other president had done before by swearing in two other presidents. Taft held the two highest offices in the land, president of the United States and chief justice of the Supreme Court.

Taft hated being president. He became grumpy, lonely, and depressed. He had a cabinet to talk to, a White House staff to attend to his every need, and fancy cars to ride around in, yet he called the White House the lonesomest place on earth. It's ironic that Taft's wife, Nellie, felt she was born to be the wife of a president, but shortly after her husband took office she had a debilitating stroke, and she spent much of her time as First Lady relearning how to do things that were once easy. She didn't get to spend enough time doing her dream job.

Taft gained almost 100 pounds during his presidency. He would often eat to vent his frustration and depression. Even though he was the heaviest U.S. president ever, he was quite physically active. He played golf so much that the sport became very popular during his time in office. He also could be found on the South Beach . . . no, definitely not the diet, but a Waikiki beach instead, learning to surf. Yes, he was one of our only surfing presidents, not to be confused with those who surfed the information highway (or World Wide Web).

Taft's most embarrassing moment had to be when he was pried out of the White House bathtub because he got stuck. The tub was immediately replaced with a tub that could hold three average-sized men. Hey, is that the rhyme that goes, "Rub-a-dub-dub, three men in a tub"?

Did You Know That . . .

★ Taft was the first president to buy a car for the White House?

★ William Taft was the president who started the tradition of throwing out the "first pitch" on the opening day of baseball?

★ President Taft's new White House tub was seven feet long and forty-one inches wide and weighed around a ton?

★ Taft loved his milk and brought his own milk cows to the White House? (The first cow's name was Wooly Mooly; she was later replaced by another favorite cow, Pauline Wayne.)

★ Taft was a wrestler in college?

★ Taft's wife, Helen, was small and very ambitious?

★ When Taft left office, he lost ninety pounds?

★ President Taft was known to fall asleep during meetings and conferences?

★ The White House horse stalls were turned into garages during Taft's administration?

★ President Taft had four cars? (A White Steamer, two Pierce-Arrows, and a Baker Electric.)

★ William Taft was the first president to pay federal income tax on his salary? (The Sixteenth Amendment was ratified in 1913.)

★ First Lady Nellie Taft was responsible for the cherry trees planted in Washington, D.C., along the Potomac?

★ New Mexico and Arizona became states during Taft's tenure?

★ The *Titanic* sank while William Taft was president?

★ The Boy Scouts became an organization during Taft's administration?

★ The Taft's cow Pauline Wayne was the last one to graze on the White House lawn?

★ Taft's funeral was the first presidential funeral to be broadcast on the radio?

★ William Taft was the first president to be buried in Arlington National Cemetery? (One of two to be buried there—he and JFK.)

★ During Taft's presidency the Indian-head penny became the Lincoln-head penny?

★ The 1912 election was the first time the primaries were used?

★ Taft was the last president to have facial hair?

★ President Taft was a seventh cousin twice removed of Richard Nixon?

★ William Taft liked to be chauffeured around in his White Steamer and doze in the backseat?

★ President Taft and former president Theodore Roosevelt were the best of friends until after Taft's term as president?

★ People made Taft's name an acronym involving Roosevelt? ("Take Advice from Teddy.")

★ When Taft was serving as the chief justice of the Supreme Court, he dedicated the Lincoln Memorial? (In 1922.)

★ Former president Taft swore two presidents into office while serving as chief justice? (Calvin Coolidge and Herbert Hoover.)

★ Taft was the first president of forty-eight states?

★ Taft was distantly related to Ralph Waldo Emerson?

★ Taft liked musical theater?

★ ★ ★ ★ ★ ★ ★ ★ ★ ★ ★ ★ ★ ★ ★

There Have Been . . .
Eighteen Republican Presidents:

ABRAHAM LINCOLN

ULYSSES S. GRANT

RUTHERFORD B. HAYES

JAMES GARFIELD

CHESTER ARTHUR

BENJAMIN HARRISON

WILLIAM MCKINLEY

THEODORE ROOSEVELT

WILLIAM TAFT

WARREN HARDING

CALVIN COOLIDGE

HERBERT HOOVER

DWIGHT EISENHOWER

RICHARD NIXON

GERALD FORD

RONALD REAGAN

GEORGE H. W. BUSH

GEORGE W. BUSH

BIRTHDAY: December 28, 1856,
in Staunton, Virginia

PARENTS: Joseph Ruggles and
Jessie Woodrow Wilson

FIRST LADIES: Ellen Louise Axson and
Edith Bolling Galt

KIDS: Margaret Woodrow, Jessie Woodrow,
and Eleanor Randolph Wilson

COLLEGES: College of New Jersey (now Princeton);
University of Virginia Law School;
Johns Hopkins University

JOBS BEFORE PRESIDENT: Lawyer, Professor,
Princeton University President,
Governor of New Jersey

POLITICAL PARTY: Democratic

RELIGION: Presbyterian

AGE AT INAUGURATION: Fifty-six

YEARS IN OFFICE: 1913–1921

NICKNAME: The Schoolmaster

DIED: February 3, 1924

Woodrow Wilson

#28

—was the studious son of a Presbyterian minister. He was the first and only president to have earned a Ph.D. He also won the Nobel Peace Prize for his efforts at peace after World War I. He tried to establish a protocol for nations to work out peaceful solutions (the League of Nations).

Wilson was also a gifted orator and used his talent in many situations during his presidency. Is this guy sounding a bit straitlaced and nerdy? Woodrow Wilson was anything but straitlaced or nerdy, especially in the *love* department. There are still in existence today over 1,000 love letters that he wrote to his wife, telling of his desire for her and his wish to be with her always. He was a hopeless romantic. The problem with this, however, was that he was this way with another woman, too; only she was not his wife. She got letters, too! His wife ultimately forgave him and he promised his faithfulness to the end. Have we heard this before?

When First Lady Ellen Wilson died, President Wilson was devastated. They had been married for twenty-nine years and had three daughters together. He mourned and mourned, so much that his doctor suggested that he needed to play golf for exercise and to get his mind off things. Wilson took up the sport reluctantly but played so much that he became a great golfer. He played even in the winter, using black golf balls in the snow. His average score is still better than most chief executives who have played the game. Even though he played very well, he never enjoyed it. Seventeen months and several golf games later, he married a Washington widow named Edith Galt. They were very close and in love, and she, like the first Mrs. Wilson, was his greatest friend and adviser. During his second term President Wilson suffered a stroke that completely incapacitated him. The severity of the stroke was not known to the public or even to his vice president. First Lady Edith Wilson handled his presidency for the remainder of his term and screened his visitors, allowing hardly anyone to see him again. She informed him of what was happening, signed documents, and sat through his meetings for him.

So you could say Edith Wilson was America's first female president, right? Is that too much credit to give her? No, it is not too much credit to give her. She deserves a lot of credit, especially since President Wilson was up in his room all day in his pj's watching over 400 movies while she was going to meetings, signing documents, and screening his calls and visitors. After President Wilson died, Edith Wilson lived another thirty-seven years.

Did You Know That . . .

★ Wilson's Ph.D. thesis was titled "Congressional Government"?

★ President Wilson was blind in one eye?

★ Woodrow Wilson was plagued with indigestion (nausea, constipation, and heartburn) since childhood and sometimes used a stomach pump?

★ President Wilson was completely blind in his last years of life?

★ Wilson was one of fifteen presidents who became president without winning the popular vote? (He won 42 percent.)

★ Wilson was the first president to cross the Atlantic Ocean while in office?

★ Wilson was the first president to hold a modern press conference?

★ The Wilson family had a pet sheep named Old Ike that chewed tobacco and grazed on the White House lawn?

★ Wilson did not learn to read until age nine (perhaps due to dyslexia)?

★ Wilson was the only president to be buried in Washington, D.C.? (Remember, Taft and JFK were buried in Arlington National Cemetery, but it is in Virginia.)

★ Edith Wilson was the first First Lady to go on an international visit to Europe?

★ Wilson's portrait appeared on the $100,000 bill? (This bill was used only for transactions between the Federal Reserve and the U.S. Treasury.)

★ Wilson loved automobiles and took a daily ride to calm himself?

★ One of the bridges over the Potomac is called the Woodrow Wilson Bridge?

★ Wilson detonated the final explosives that cleared the Panama Canal? (He gave the signal from New York.)

★ President Wilson ended child labor?

★ Woodrow Wilson served on the faculties of Wesleyan University, Bryn Mawr College, and Princeton University?

★ During Wilson's presidency the United States declared war on Germany and began U.S. involvement in World War I?

★ Wilson proposed the League of Nations to help with his peace plan after World War I?

★ The United States never joined the League of Nations because Wilson refused to negotiate with the Senate on certain aspects of the deal?

★ The Nineteenth Amendment was ratified and women won the right to vote in 1920? (Wilson was not in favor of this, ladies.)

★ Wilson's children would wear disguises to leave the White House and sightsee in Washington?

★ President Wilson did his own typing? (His typewriter could type English and Greek.)

★ Wilson considered 13 to be his lucky number? (It was also the number of letters in his name.)

★ Wilson had few male friends and his wives were his closest friends and advisers?

★ Woodrow Wilson was the second Democratic president to serve after the Civil War?

★ Wilson's reelection was the first Democratic president's reelection since Andrew Jackson's?

★ President Wilson's handshake was limp and lifeless?

★ Sigmund Freud authored a psychological biography of Woodrow Wilson? (It was published in 1967.)

★ Woodrow Wilson's first childhood memory was of hearing at age four that Abraham Lincoln had been elected president?

★ Woodrow Wilson was called Tommy all through his childhood? (His first name was Thomas.)

★ Wilson was the first president to travel to European soil?

★ Wilson was the last president who remembered the Civil War?

★ President Wilson proclaimed the very first Flag Day? (Flag Day is still celebrated today.)

★ President Wilson's last words were "I am ready"?

★ Woodrow Wilson was the first president to join AAA (the American Automobile Association)?

★ President Wilson was a great bridge player?

★ Wilson was five feet eleven inches tall and weighed between 175 and 185 pounds?

BIRTHDAY: November 2, 1865,
in Blooming Grove, Ohio

PARENTS: George Tyron and
Phoebe Elizabeth Dickerson Harding

FIRST LADY: Florence Mabel Kling DeWolfe

KIDS: None (but several rumored illegitimate children)

COLLEGE: Iberia College
(now Ohio Central College)

JOBS BEFORE PRESIDENT: Teacher,
Insurance Salesman, Editor-Publisher,
Ohio State Senator, Lieutenant
Governor of Ohio, U.S. Senator

POLITICAL PARTY: Republican

RELIGION: Baptist

AGE AT INAUGURATION: Fifty-five

YEARS IN OFFICE: 1921–1923

NICKNAME: Wobbly Warren

DIED: August 2, 1923

Warren Gamaliel Harding

#29

—played the sousaphone and lots of poker and was a member of the Ku Klux Klan. He was popular, especially with the ladies, and we are not talking about the First Lady, either. Harding was once the young owner/publisher of the *Marion Star* newspaper in Ohio. He had absolutely loved his time there and with the help of his wife built the paper into a huge financial success. His love of the newspaper business made him automatically popular with the press during his presidency.

President Harding was known to have frequent White House poker games. These games were with his buddies who were known as the "poker cabinet." Sometimes Mrs. Harding would be the bartender for the weekly event. The guys would smoke, drink, and gamble the night away. There was one particular game in which the president gambled big and lost, only this time it was a "historic" loss that he would receive a lot of flak over: President Harding had gambled away an entire set of White House china in one of his famous poker games. He also played a lot of golf—anything to get him out of the office. He didn't like to work too hard.

Speaking of china, President Harding's name would become linked with one of the biggest scandals of presidential history, the Teapot Dome Scandal. His secretary of the interior had illegally leased navy oil reserves in California and Wyoming to wealthy oilmen in exchange for kickbacks (money and lots of it). There was no evidence that Harding knew about this or received any money, but he was ultimately responsible. His entire cabinet was corrupt and brought down any good that Harding might have accomplished during his administration.

Harding was having health problems and decided to take a few trips and combine vacationing with campaigning for reelection. He died while traveling, and many people accused his wife of poisoning him so that he would not have to endure the scandals that were being revealed daily about his affairs, his corrupt cabinet, and the Teapot Dome Scandal.

Did You Know That . . .

★ Warren Harding was one of seven presidents from Ohio?

★ Harding campaigned from his front porch?

★ Harding was the first presidential candidate to hire a speechwriter?

★ Earlier in Harding's life he suffered a nervous breakdown and spent time in a sanitarium in Michigan?

★ Harding's presidency is ranked as one of the worst by historians?

★ Harding was the first president to ride to his inauguration in a car?

★ Harding had a pet dog that sat in his very own chair at cabinet meetings? (His name was Laddie Boy.)

★ Harding had a birthday party for Laddie Boy and had a cake made of dog biscuits for him?

★ Harding was the first president to speak over the radio?

★ Harding was the first president to visit Canada?

★ Harding had a pet canary named Bob?

★ Harding was the first president to have a golf course named after him?

★ Harding's mom called him Winnie?

★ Harding wore a whopping size-14 shoe, making him the president with the biggest feet?

★ Harding had several affairs, yet his wife forgave him?

★ President Harding kept the White House stocked with bootleg liquor even though as an Ohio senator he had voted for Prohibition?

★ Harding attended baseball games regularly?

★ Florence Harding was the very first First Lady to get to vote for her husband for president?

★ President Harding's wife solicited the help of many former First Ladies to help her in a campaign to help veterans? (The group became known as Flossie's Gang.)

★ Harding served alcohol to his friends and family and was breaking the law because Prohibition made it illegal?

★ President Harding missed several very important Senate meetings because he did not want to argue?

★ Harding owned so many clothes that closets had to be added in the White House?

★ President Harding liked to play Ping-Pong?

★ Harding's dog, Laddie Boy, delivered daily newspapers to his master?

★ Harding's wife, who was known as overbearing and "in charge," was sometimes called "the Duchess"?

★ President Harding once shook 7,000 people's hands at one event?

★ Harding was credited with coining the term "normalcy"?

★ Harding was the first sitting senator to be elected president?

★ President Harding was six feet tall?

★ Harding had white hair and thick black eyebrows?

★ Harding had at least one illegitimate child?

★ ★ ★ ★ ★ ★ ★ ★ ★ ★ ★ ★ ★ ★ ★ ★

There Have Never Been More Than Five Former Presidents Living at the Same Time

- *March 4, 1861–January 18, 1862:*
  Martin Van Buren, John Tyler, Millard Fillmore, Franklin Pierce, and James Buchanan were all alive during the Lincoln administration until John Tyler died.

- *January 20, 1993–April 22, 1994:*
  Richard Nixon, Gerald Ford, Jimmy Carter, Ronald Reagan, and George H. W. Bush were all alive during the Clinton administration until Richard Nixon died.

- *January 20, 2001–June 5, 2004:*
  Gerald Ford, Jimmy Carter, Ronald Reagan, George H. W. Bush, and Bill Clinton were all alive during the first administration of George W. Bush until Ronald Reagan died.

BIRTHDAY: July 4, 1872, in Plymouth, Vermont

PARENTS: John Calvin and
Victoria Josephine Moor Coolidge

FIRST LADY: Grace Anna Goodhue

KIDS: John and Calvin (1908–1924) Coolidge

COLLEGE: Amherst College

JOBS BEFORE PRESIDENT: Lawyer, City Councilman,
Member of Massachusetts State Legislature, Mayor,
Massachusetts State Senator, Lieutenant Governor
of Massachusetts, Governor of Massachusetts,
Vice President under Warren Harding

POLITICAL PARTY: Republican

RELIGION: Congregationalist

AGE AT INAUGURATION: Fifty

YEARS IN OFFICE: 1923–1929

NICKNAME: Silent Cal

DIED: January 5, 1933

Calvin Coolidge

#30

—was the president who needed the most sleep. He slept more than ten hours a day and took an afternoon nap as well. "Silent Cal" Coolidge was a very different kind of guy. He had a mechanical horse installed in his bedroom in the White House. He would ride it each evening for exercise. His Secret Service agents enjoyed it as well. One of the weirdest habits of this commander in chief was his morning routine. He enjoyed having his head rubbed with Vaseline while he ate breakfast in bed. Okay, if he is sleeping ten hours a day, and having his head rubbed with petroleum jelly while eating breakfast in bed, the question comes to mind: When did he get any work done?

Before his election in 1924, Coolidge's younger son, Calvin junior, developed a blister while playing tennis on the White House courts. The blister became infected, and Calvin junior died. After that, Coolidge, a man of few words who had already earned the nickname Silent Cal, became more withdrawn.

He was so quiet and stoic that it frustrated the press on a regular basis. They would ask him if he had information about the world situation, Prohibition, the campaign, and his response would always be a one-word answer: "No." The press conferences were looked at as a joke. As a final act of sarcasm Coolidge would remind each reporter not to quote him.

Everyone knew that President Coolidge was an extremely quiet and reserved man. Once, during a state dinner, the lady seated next to him told him that she had bet another friend that she could make him say more than two words. He turned to her and simply replied, "You lose." He said nothing else for the entire evening.

Did You Know That . . .

★ Calvin Coolidge played the harmonica?

★ President Coolidge brought his own rocking chair with him to the White House?

★ Coolidge was always trying to sneak past his Secret Service guards so that he could take a walk by himself? (He never could.)

★ President Coolidge could be found at night wandering around the Executive Mansion in his nightshirt?

★ Calvin Coolidge's father swore him into office when he received the news of Harding's death? (The swearing-in was at 2:45 A.M.)

★ In an attempt to be frugal, President Coolidge raised chickens at the White House?

★ The Coolidges' dog was named Paul Pry?

★ The Coolidges also had a pet raccoon that they walked regularly on a leash?

★ President Coolidge's cat, Tiger, kept running away? (They put out radio bulletins about their missing cat. He would be found but would run away again and again.)

★ President Coolidge was a practical joker and would play pranks on the White House staff?

★ President Coolidge vetoed a farm relief bill? (This bill could have helped prevent the Great Depression.)

★ Coolidge was a very visible president—he held regular press conferences, spoke on the radio, and posed for portraits dressed in farmer overalls, cowboy hats, chaps, full Indian headdresses, and Boy Scout uniforms?

★ President Coolidge loved Cuban cigars?

★ Coolidge's vice president, Charles Dawes, earned a Nobel Peace Prize?

★ First Lady Grace Coolidge was a teacher of the deaf who taught the whole family sign language?

★ Sometimes the Coolidges spoke in sign language when they didn't want anyone to understand their conversation?

★ President Coolidge had a donkey named Ebeneezer and a goose that had starred in a Broadway play?

★ President Coolidge would not use the phone while he was in office?

★ Calvin Coolidge was one of two presidents from Vermont?

★ Coolidge's inaugural speech was forty-one minutes long and broadcast on twenty-five radio stations that ultimately reached over 22 million people?

★ President Coolidge kept his dog's drinking bowl in the state dining room?

★ President Coolidge suffered from asthma, hay fever, bronchitis, and upset stomach?

★ Calvin Coolidge was born on the Fourth of July? (He was the only president who was born on that day.)

★ Calvin Coolidge's last words were "Good morning, Robert"?

★ Each time that President Coolidge rode in an automobile, he asked that the driver not go any faster than 16 mph?

★ Calvin Coolidge's first name was John?

★ President Coolidge lit the very first National Christmas Tree on the Ellipse? (An area of the White House South Lawn.)

★ During Coolidge's presidency Walt Disney created the very first Mickey Mouse cartoon, called "Steamboat Willie"?

★ Coolidge was the only president to have his face on a U.S. coin while living? (The 1926 sesquicentennial half-dollar.)

★ President Coolidge was five feet nine inches tall?

★ In retirement Coolidge spoke on the radio airwaves and warned listeners to beware of insurance agents adjusting their policies?

★ An insurance agent sued Coolidge for $100,000 because he had lost business due to Coolidge's speech? (Coolidge settled out of court for $2,500.)

★ Coolidge died of heart complications and left his $700,000 estate to his wife?

BIRTHDAY: August 10, 1874,
in West Branch, Iowa

PARENTS: Jesse Clark and
Hulda Randall Minthorn Hoover

FIRST LADY: Lou Henry

KIDS: Herbert Clark and Allan Henry Hoover

COLLEGE: Stanford University

JOBS BEFORE PRESIDENT: Mining Engineer,
Public Administrator, Secretary of Commerce
under Warren Harding, Secretary of
Commerce under Calvin Coolidge

POLITICAL PARTY: Republican

RELIGION: Quaker

AGE AT INAUGURATION: Fifty-four

YEARS IN OFFICE: 1929–1933

NICKNAME: The Great Engineer

DIED: October 20, 1964

Herbert Hoover

#31

—was in the right place at the wrong time. It was the Great Depression and *he* was president. The Depression was not Hoover's fault and had been building slowly through several administrations. His nervous and shy personality truly failed him during these years because he was not effective at speaking to the American people or encouraging them. It didn't help that Hoover was a millionaire and the rest of America was starving. The Hoovers carried on in the White House as if nothing was wrong, serving seven-course formal-dress meals even when the president and the First Lady dined alone.

The White House physician, Dr. Joel T. Boone, wanted President Hoover to exercise more. In order for the president to do so Dr. Boone created a game now known as Hoover-ball. It required less skill than tennis and was more aerobic. It was a combination of tennis and volleyball, and like using a medicine ball. The press had reported that it was more strenuous than boxing, wrestling, or football. Hoover-ball was played with two to four players, one six-pound medicine ball, and a volleyball net. The game was scored just like tennis. The server began by throwing the ball over the net, and the opposing team had to try to catch it and send it back over. The team that missed first or threw out-of-bounds lost the point. The difficulty and challenge in this game was catching the six-pound ball with speed behind it. Hoover's doctor came up with different versions of the game to keep him fit. He would play with his cabinet members and VIPs, who would show up at the time each morning's game would begin. They rarely stopped these morning games for weather. The game was played rain or shine.

President and Mrs. Hoover were mining engineers. They were experts in geology and metals. They both graduated from Stanford University. The School of Engineering at Columbia University conducted a survey in 1964 regarding the greatest engineers of all time. Herbert Hoover and Thomas Edison were selected as the best in United States history.

When Hoover ran for reelection, he traveled by train a lot to campaign. At one stop in the Midwest, Americans hurled tomatoes and eggs at his train car. He would not be reelected and his legacy would be the Great Depression. Maybe this is why Hoover was sometimes greatly depressed himself.

Did You Know That . . .

★ Herbert Hoover was the very first president born west of the Mississippi?

★ Hoover promised America's voters "a chicken in every pot and a car in every garage"?

★ Herbert Hoover was an orphan at age nine?

★ Eight months after President Hoover took office, the stock market crashed?

★ During the Hoover administration homeless people lived in little shantytowns (consisting of cardboard shacks) called Hoovervilles?

★ During Hoover's administration the planet Pluto was first discovered?

★ During Hoover's term Amelia Earhart became the first woman to fly solo across the Atlantic Ocean?

★ President Hoover's son Allan had two pet alligators in the White House, and sometimes they wandered around the Executive Mansion?

★ During Hoover's administration "The Star-Spangled Banner" became the national anthem? (Hoover officially selected it.)

★ When the Hoovers didn't want anyone to hear their conversations, they spoke in Chinese?

★ President Hoover did not accept his salary when he was president? (He spent his own money to entertain.)

★ President Hoover was a great fisherman, loved to fly-fish, and wrote a book on fishing called *Fishing for Fun—to Wash Your Soul*?

★ President Hoover had honorary degrees from fifty universities?

★ Hoover had become a millionaire by age forty?

★ The Hoovers had traveled around the world extensively? (They found gold in Australia and China. They were millionaires several times over.)

★ President Hoover established UNICEF? (The international children's fund.)

★ President Hoover was a Quaker and used the word "affirm" instead of "swear" when taking the presidential oath of office?

★ Hoover was the first president to have an asteroid named after him?

★ Hoover's secretary of state won a Nobel Peace Prize?

★ Herbert Hoover was one of four presidents to live past his ninetieth birthday?

★ Hoover never held an elected office before being president?

★ Hoover was distantly related to Richard Nixon? (Eighth cousin once removed.)

★ Charles Curtis was the first person of Kaw Indian descent to be elected to the vice presidency?

★ Hoover was the last president to have his term end on March 3?

★ Hoover was the first president to have a telephone on his desk in the White House?

★ White House staff and groundskeepers were given orders by President Hoover to hide when he and his wife passed by? (If they didn't, they could lose their jobs.)

★ President Hoover lived out his retirement years in the fancy Waldorf Towers in New York City? (His library has a replica of the apartment.)

★ President Hoover was five feet eleven inches tall?

★ Hoover was deaf and blind at the end of his life?

★ ★ ★ ★ ★ ★ ★ ★ ★ ★ ★ ★ ★ ★ ★ ★

Presidential Potpourri

- President William Howard Taft could have been a pitcher for the Cincinnati Reds.

- Three presidents have been sons of ministers: Chester Arthur, Grover Cleveland, and Woodrow Wilson.

- President George Washington was the first person to breed roses in the United States. Washington created a garden of his own rose selections at Mount Vernon.

- Jimmy Carter brought five jumbo rockers to the White House. They were his favorites, designed by Thomas Brumby in 1875.

- Abraham Lincoln paid $2,600 for a set of pearls with matching earrings from Tiffany's for his wife, Mary.

★

The president's address is:
The President
1600 Pennsylvania Avenue, NW
Washington, D.C. 20500

The president's e-mail address is:
president@whitehouse.gov

BIRTHDAY: January 30, 1882,
in Hyde Park, New York

PARENTS: James and Sara Delano Roosevelt

FIRST LADY: Anna Eleanor Roosevelt

KIDS: Anna Eleanor, James, Franklin Delano
(born and died 1909), Elliott, Franklin Delano,
and John Aspinwall Roosevelt

COLLEGES: Harvard; Columbia Law School

JOBS BEFORE PRESIDENT: Lawyer, Banker,
New York State Senator, Member of New York State
Legislature, Assistant Secretary of the Navy under
Woodrow Wilson, Governor of New York

POLITICAL PARTY: Democratic

RELIGION: Episcopalian

AGE AT INAUGURATION: Fifty-one

YEARS IN OFFICE: 1933–1945

NICKNAMES: FDR; The New Dealer

DIED: April 12, 1945

Franklin Delano Roosevelt

#32

—was thirty-nine years old when he was stricken with polio. That day FDR had been sailing and fishing with his family. He had assisted some neighbors in fighting a fire and had even gone swimming right afterward. He jogged home (about a mile) in his swim trunks. That evening he went to bed feeling sick and he had the chills. Several days later he couldn't move his legs. Though depressed and angry about what was happening to him, FDR fought back through exercise and rehabilitation. He visited Warm Springs, a rehabilitation spa in Georgia, regularly. He never regained the use of his legs but did get them strong enough to stand with braces and even walk with crutches or a cane. He usually used a wheelchair that he made himself out of a kitchen chair. Roosevelt's handicap was hidden from the public. He was rarely photographed getting in or out of automobiles or in his wheelchair. Roosevelt was conscious of the fragile state of America during the Depression and wanted Americans to have full confidence in their leader.

Speaking of leaders, it was almost a glimpse into the future when Franklin Roosevelt met President Cleveland. FDR's father took him to the White House to meet the sitting president. When five-year-old Franklin Roosevelt was introduced to President Grover Cleveland, the president gave FDR this advice: "My little man, I am making a strange wish for you. It is that you may never be president of the United States." Hmmm.

President Franklin Roosevelt had a special room known as the Fish Room. It was located just outside the president's office in the White House. This room served as a sort of waiting room for guests. All of the president's fishing memorabilia were displayed on the walls and mementos from his favorite fishing trips could be found around the room. FDR was sometimes known to reminisce with guests about his different fishing experiences and proudly show off the items in the room. The room was rectangular in shape, had no windows, and housed a large fish tank. The room also functioned as a conference room. A skylight was added in later years and Nixon renamed it the Roosevelt Room in honor of Franklin Delano and Theodore Roosevelt.

Roosevelt had a hobby of collecting stamps—postage stamps, that is, of all shapes and sizes. He became "stuck on stamps" when he was eleven years old and collected throughout his lifetime. He is said to have owned over forty albums full of over 25,000 stamps. As chief executive he was sent the very first sheet of every new commemorative stamp. His friends, staff, and even cabinet would often help add to his collection when they traveled and found un- usual stamps. His hobby took his mind off the Great Depression and the pressures of being president. He was a great example of really committing to something and "sticking" to it!

Did You Know That . . .

★ At FDR's first inauguration to the presidency he had two grandchildren; when his second inauguration came around, he had thirteen grandchildren?

★ Roosevelt was the only president elected to four terms? (He died in office during his fourth term.)

★ First Lady Eleanor Roosevelt was an orphan by age ten? (She was raised by her grandmother.)

★ President and Mrs. Roosevelt were distant (fifth) cousins?

★ During World War II, First Lady Eleanor Roosevelt visited American soldiers in Europe?

★ Eleanor Roosevelt traveled all over America speaking to people about her husband's plans?

★ First Lady Eleanor Roosevelt wrote a newspaper column and held many press conferences on women's rights?

★ Even though FDR was paralyzed, he traveled more than any president up to his time?

★ President Roosevelt exercised regularly by swimming and by crawling with his hands around the house?

★ Roosevelt's favorite writer was Mark Twain?

★ Franklin Roosevelt had a loyal companion in his dog, Fala, who went everywhere with him?

★ Once, aboard a U.S. ship, a crewman clipped off some of Fala's hair for a souvenir?

★ FDR wrestled with his sons, sometimes two at a time?

★ President Roosevelt appointed the first female cabinet member? (Frances Perkins, secretary of labor.)

★ FDR loved to play poker?

★ Franklin Roosevelt's mom, Sara Delano Roosevelt, was the first woman to vote for her son for president?

★ First Lady Eleanor Roosevelt refused Secret Service protection; she drove her own car and the Secret Service made her keep a pistol in the glove compartment?

★ President Roosevelt used to scramble eggs for friends in the White House kitchen? (He loved scrambled eggs.)

★ The very first dishwasher and bomb shelter were added to the White House during FDR's term?

★ Roosevelt was the first president to appear on television?

★ FDR was the first president to have a presidential aircraft?

★ President Roosevelt's favorite sport was swimming?

★ "Home on the Range" was Roosevelt's favorite song?

★ FDR met with the press over 975 times during his presidency?

★ In 1939, when the king and queen of England visited, he served them hot dogs?

★ FDR discontinued the famous Easter Egg Roll at the White House for eleven years?

★ President Roosevelt kept a future president out of prison for tax fraud? (Lyndon B. Johnson.)

★ Franklin Roosevelt had a record 935 vetoes and Congress overturned only 10 of them?

★ The first time FDR voted, he voted for Theodore Roosevelt?

★ Sometimes President Roosevelt called his wife, Eleanor, "Granny" (a childhood nickname)?

★ President Roosevelt had a longtime mistress?

★ FDR smoked cigarettes (a pack a day)?

★ Roosevelt was the first president to visit South America and Hawaii during his presidency?

★ President Roosevelt encouraged Americans through weekly radio addresses known as the Fireside Chats during the war and the Depression?

★ FDR created Social Security to provide senior citizens with a pension to survive on, as well as those who were disabled?

★ FDR created large federal economic and welfare programs called the New Deal?

★ Roosevelt had to get rid of his German shepherd named Major because he bit almost everyone?

★ Copy machines were invented, the Golden Gate Bridge was dedicated, and nylon was developed during Roosevelt's term?

★ FDR wore dresses as a young child?

★ Franklin Roosevelt had been the vice presidential candidate for James Cox, who ran against Warren Harding?

★ President Roosevelt dedicated the Thomas Jefferson Memorial in Washington, D.C., in 1943?

★ John A. Roosevelt, FDR's youngest son, was the only son who became a member of the Republican Party?

★ Eleanor Roosevelt escaped in a lifeboat with her parents when the HMS *Britannic* sank? (She was only three.)

★ FDR's face was put on the U.S. dime currency in 1946?

★ Eleanor's first name was actually Anna?

★ ★ ★ ★ ★ ★ ★ ★ ★ ★ ★ ★ ★ ★ ★ ★ ★

Presidential Potpourri

• Presidents' Day was originally celebrated as two different U.S. presidents' birthdays: George Washington's and Abraham Lincoln's.

• Today Presidents' Day celebrates all presidents of the United States. Richard Nixon declared Washington's birthday "Presidents' Day" in 1971.

★

• The president is the commander in chief of the armed forces.

• The president nominates Supreme Court justices, negotiates treaties with other countries, and appoints U.S. ambassadors to other countries.

• The president has the power to grant a full or conditional pardon (the only exception is in the case of impeachment).

BIRTHDAY: May 8, 1884, in Lamar, Missouri

PARENTS: John Anderson and
Martha Ellen Young Truman

FIRST LADY: Elizabeth Virginia ("Bess") Wallace

KID: Mary Margaret Truman

COLLEGES: Spalding's Commercial College;
University of Kansas City School of Law

JOBS BEFORE PRESIDENT: Clerk, Salesman,
Farmer, Soldier, Judge, U.S. Senator,
Vice President under Franklin D. Roosevelt

POLITICAL PARTY: Democratic

RELIGION: Baptist

AGE AT INAUGURATION: Sixty

YEARS IN OFFICE: 1945–1953

NICKNAME: Give 'Em Hell Harry

DIED: December 26, 1972

Harry S. Truman

#33

—read his December 6, 1950, *Washington Post* and began to fume! There was a music review of his only daughter Margaret Truman's vocal concert. The critic's name, Paul Hume, will live in infamy for stating that Margaret was "extremely attractive" but that "Miss Truman cannot sing very well and has not improved over the years." The president was full of rage and wrote several drafts of a letter to Mr. Hume. He strategized how to get this letter past his advisers and into the U.S. mail. He simply stamped it, took a walk, and mailed it himself. Here is what he wrote to Paul Hume:

Mr. Hume:

I've just read your lousy review of Margaret's concert. I've come to the conclusion that you are an "eight ulcer man on four ulcer pay."

It seems to me that you are a frustrated old man who wishes he could have been successful. When you write such poppy-cock as was in the back section of the paper you work for it shows conclusively that you're off the beam and at least four of your ulcers are at work.

Some day I hope to meet you. When that happens you'll need a new nose, a lot of beefsteak for black eyes, and perhaps a supporter below!

Pegler, a gutter snipe, is a gentleman alongside you. I hope you'll accept that statement as a worse insult than a reflection on your ancestry.

H.S.T.

Truman's mother was equally as colorful as her son. Martha Ellen Young Truman held a grudge forever against the Union because some of her ancestors were forced to do time in a Union internment camp. She declared herself a Confederate to the end. Even when her son was elected president, she didn't change her tune. He invited her for a visit to the White House. When the president's mom was shown to the Lincoln Bedroom to sleep for the night, she told everyone that she would rather sleep on the floor than in Mr. Lincoln's bed.

Harry Truman had to be so tired of the "buck stops here" thing. Finishing FDR's term and completing one of his own, he had to end a war, declare a war, observe the beginnings of the Vietnam War, drop an atomic bomb, try to stamp out communism, and defend his daughter's singing career. . . . Whew!

Did You Know That . . .

★ Harry Truman was playing a poker game when he found out he was going to be the president?

★ Truman was the first president to travel underwater in a new modern submarine?

★ Harry Truman's middle name was S.? (It really didn't stand for anything. The "S" represented both of his grandfathers, whose names had an "S" in them.)

★ Truman's secretary of state won a Nobel Peace Prize?

★ Truman was briefed about the atomic bomb for only thirty minutes?

★ Truman loved to play the piano?

★ Harry Truman was the great-great-great-nephew of former president John Tyler?

★ Harry Truman was the first president to receive a salary of $100,000?

★ President Truman was left-handed?

★ Truman had been a captain in the field artillery in World War I?

★ Truman was famous for saying, "If you can't stand the heat, get out of the kitchen"?

★ Truman was named one of the ten best-dressed senators?

★ Harry Truman was the first president to take office during wartime?

★ Truman was one of fifteen presidents who did not win the majority of the popular vote but became president?

★ President Truman redesigned the presidential seal?

★ Truman had a pet goat named Dewey's Goat?

★ First Lady Bess Truman had all of her family's laundry sent back to Independence, Missouri, to be laundered because she didn't like the laundry services in Washington, D.C.?

★ Truman liked white wine and bourbon?

★ Harry Truman didn't smoke?

★ Truman met Bess in Sunday school when they were six years old?

★ President Harry Truman walked two miles each morning and kept a 128-steps-per-minute pace?

★ During Truman's administration the Twenty-second Amendment to the Constitution was ratified, stating that "no person shall be elected to the office of the President more than twice"?

★ Harry Truman read every book in his hometown library of Independence, Missouri, by age fifteen?

★ During Truman's administration Jackie Robinson became the first African American to play major-league baseball?

★ The Korean War began in 1950, during Harry Truman's second term in office?

★ President Truman had to make the difficult decision of using atomic weapons against Japan?

★ Harry Truman wanted to end segregation and racial discrimination?

★ First Lady Bess Truman loved baseball and tried to go to as many games as possible?

★ President Truman was the only twentieth-century president who didn't get a college degree? (He attended college and law school classes but never graduated.)

★ The Truman family lived in the Blair House (normally reserved for state guests) from 1949 to 1952, while the White House was receiving some much-needed renovations?

★ Truman was so nervous when he was taking the oath of office, he had to read it from a piece of paper?

★ When the House of Representatives wanted to award the Congressional Medal of Honor to former president Harry Truman on his eighty-seventh birthday, he refused, saying that he had done nothing to deserve it?

★ President Truman gave the very first televised presidential address to the nation?

★ Truman had owned a men's clothing store before becoming president?

★ First Lady Bess Truman wrote many of her husband's speeches?

★ Truman was the first former president to formally address the Senate? (On his eightieth birthday.)

★ Harry Truman owned over a dozen tailor-made suits that showed off his trim physical condition?

★ President Truman hosted the very first televised White House tour?

★ As a result of the White House renovations that were done during the Truman administration, the Treasury Department had to engrave new $20 bills? (The backs of the bills needed to reflect the new porch on the White House.)

★ Harry Truman described the music of "The Star-Spangled Banner" as "bad"?

★ President Truman described in his memoirs that being the president was like riding a tiger?

★ President Truman sometimes described the White House as "a nice prison but a prison"?

★ Truman was five feet eleven inches tall and weighed around 185 pounds?

★ Truman's daughter, Margaret, is the author of the best-selling book *The President's House* and a number of best-selling mystery novels?

★ ★ ★ ★ ★ ★ ★ ★ ★ ★ ★ ★ ★ ★ ★ ★

Presidential Potpourri

There are three main parts of the U.S. government:

The Legislative Branch
The Executive Branch
The Judicial Branch

The Legislative Branch

- Congress (the House and Senate) makes the laws of the U.S. government.

- The House has 435 members; the Senate has 100 members (2 from each state).

- House of Representatives terms are two years; Senate terms are six years.

The Executive Branch

- President, vice president, and cabinet.

The Judicial Branch

- Federal courts. Explains and applies the laws of the U.S. government.

BIRTHDAY: October 14, 1890, in Denison, Texas

PARENTS: David Jacob and
Ida Elizabeth Stover Eisenhower

FIRST LADY: Marie Gevena ("Mamie") Doud

KIDS: Doud Dwight (1917–1921) and
John Sheldon Doud Eisenhower

COLLEGE: U.S. Military Academy at West Point

JOBS BEFORE PRESIDENT: Soldier, Author,
President of Columbia University

POLITICAL PARTY: Republican

RELIGION: Presbyterian

AGE AT INAUGURATION: Sixty-two

YEARS IN OFFICE: 1953–1961

NICKNAME: Ike

DIED: March 28, 1969

Dwight David Eisenhower

#34

—was a five-star general in the U.S. Army and the only chief executive to serve in both World War I and World War II. With this type of impressive military leadership and service you wouldn't think that his favorite hobbies were paint-by-numbers and playing canasta and bridge with his wife and friends, would you? Would you also not believe that First Lady Mamie Eisenhower enjoyed sleeping late, staying in her robe all day, and watching soap operas? This exciting leader of the free world and his wife loved watching television while eating TV dinners.

Ike was popular and trusted by the American people. They considered him the most deserving man for the job of president. In fact, he was so popular and loved that when he had a heart attack while in office, the stock market lost $14 billion that day.

Eisenhower had a total of seven heart attacks in his lifetime. Though he had heart trouble throughout his adult life, his heart always belonged to Mamie. There were rumors of an affair with his female driver during the war, but nothing has been proven. When away during his military service, he wrote Mamie not only regularly but sometimes every day, expressing his love and once sending her 100,483,491,342 kisses in one letter.

Golf was Dwight Eisenhower's passion. It is estimated that he played the game a total of 150 days a year during his two terms. The coolest thing he did was have a putting green installed on the grounds of the White House so that he could practice his swing the other 200 or so days of the year. There was only one problem: The putting green attracted every squirrel in the Washington, D.C., area. Eisenhower was tired of the varmints invading and destroying his precious green. He handled the problem with a military-type strategy and had the Secret Service devise a plan to eliminate them. The plan was called Operation Squirrel Seduction, which later turned into the final plan, known as Operation Exodus.

Did You Know That . . .

★ Dwight Eisenhower changed his first and middle names in order to avoid confusion between his name and his father's name?

★ Eisenhower was one of three presidents to graduate from a military academy? (West Point.)

★ Eisenhower was the first president of all fifty states?

★ Eisenhower was the first president to appear on color television?

★ Dwight Eisenhower carried three types of coins with him for good luck: a silver dollar, a French franc, and a five-guinea gold piece?

★ President Eisenhower was an excellent chef and had a kitchen put in the family quarters of the White House so that he could cook?

★ Eisenhower's favorite dessert was prune whip?

★ Dwight Eisenhower was the first president to be a licensed pilot?

★ President Eisenhower added "under God" to the Pledge of Allegiance?

★ Eisenhower was one of two presidents born in Texas?

★ Dwight Eisenhower played football in college and was injured trying to tackle Jim Thorpe?

★ Dwight Eisenhower was in charge of the D-day invasion of World War II?

★ Eisenhower was the first presidential nominee to travel by aircraft while on the campaign trail?

★ Eisenhower was the first president to be baptized after taking office?

★ Dwight Eisenhower was the first president to have his press conferences recorded by newsreel and television?

★ Eisenhower was the first president to be submerged in an atomic-powered submarine? (U.S.S. *Seawolf.*)

★ Dwight Eisenhower was the first president to score a hole in one in a golf game? (February 6, 1968, Palm Springs, California.)

★ President and Mrs. Eisenhower were the first First Couple to begin the tradition of sending White House Christmas cards to the public?

★ Eisenhower received many demerits for smoking (four packs a day) while in military school?

★ First Lady Mamie Eisenhower would stop whatever task she was doing each day in order to watch the soap opera *As the World Turns*?

★ First Lady Mamie Eisenhower began a Christmas tradition of serving food and giving gifts to their personal White House staff?

★ The Eisenhowers loved their dogs, Heidi and Spunky?

★ Alaska and Hawaii became the forty-ninth and fiftieth states while Dwight Eisenhower was in office?

★ During Eisenhower's administration the Supreme Court declared segregated schools unconstitutional?

★ President Eisenhower signed the bill that created the National Aeronautics and Space Administration (NASA)?

★ President Eisenhower came up with the National System of Interstate and Defense Highways, which created the largest public works program in U.S. history?

★ Eisenhower was the first president to have an exclusive presidential jet?

★ Eisenhower changed the presidential retreat's name from Shangri-La to Camp David in honor of his grandson?

★ Eisenhower wrote a book called *Crusade in Europe* and earned over $475,000?

★ Eisenhower's face was on the front of the 1971 dollar coin, and the 1969 moon landing was on the back?

★ *Time* magazine declared Dwight Eisenhower its "Man of the Year" in 1944 and 1959?

★ Dwight Eisenhower was the first chief executive to use helicopters for short presidential trips?

★ President Eisenhower's chef specialties were gourmet steak and vegetable soup?

★ Eisenhower began the interdenominational White House Prayer Breakfasts?

★ Dwight Eisenhower was the first chief executive to use makeup for his television appearances?

★ President Eisenhower had a piano put in the presidential airplane to keep First Lady Mamie Eisenhower's mind off her fear of flying?

★ Dwight Eisenhower stood five feet ten inches tall and weighed almost 180 pounds?

★ President Eisenhower had blue eyes?

★ President Eisenhower was made fun of as a kid for wearing his mom's old shoes and hand-me-down clothes?

BIRTHDAY: May 29, 1917,
in Brookline, Massachusetts

PARENTS: Joseph Patrick and
Rose Elizabeth Fitzgerald Kennedy

FIRST LADY: Jacqueline Lee Bouvier

KIDS: Caroline Bouvier, Patrick Bouvier
(born and died 1963), and John Fitzgerald Kennedy

COLLEGES: Harvard; Stanford University
Graduate School of Business Administration

JOBS BEFORE PRESIDENT: Author,
U.S. Naval Officer, Journalist,
Congressman, U.S. Senator

POLITICAL PARTY: Democratic

RELIGION: Roman Catholic

AGE AT INAUGURATION: Forty-three

YEARS IN OFFICE: 1961–1963

NICKNAMES: JFK; Jack

DIED: November 22, 1963

John Fitzgerald Kennedy

#35

—and his wife, Jacqueline Kennedy, were the movie stars of the White House. They were famous for their charm, youth, and good looks. It was as if they were the lead characters of a major motion picture and the White House became their stage. Everyone wanted to be like them, dress like them, and look like them. Jackie became a fashion icon for all women in America, and "Jack" became the focus of all women in America.

John Kennedy became a navy commander. This is kind of funny, because since childhood this future president had nothing but health problems. The military is very selective about their standards for healthy men and women. Kennedy had a history of bronchitis, tonsillitis, appendicitis, scarlet fever, measles, whooping cough, Addison's disease, back problems, abdominal pain, and fever. . . . Whew! Somehow he got into the navy and earned his way to commander. His PT boat was rammed by a Japanese destroyer. Two of the crew members died instantly. There were eleven survivors. Jack took one injured crewman's life-vest strap in his teeth and he swam for hours before they were rescued. He himself was injured in the ordeal and was given two medals for heroism and bravery.

The Kennedy family had lots of fun pets in the White House but the absolute coolest was Caroline's pony, Macaroni. Vice President Lyndon Johnson had given Macaroni to Caroline as a gift. Every kid in America wanted to meet and ride Macaroni. Sometimes the pony would roam around the White House grounds looking for Caroline or any other family members who would offer a treat. This special pony received thousands of letters from kids all across America. The Kennedy kids loved to ride in their sled pulled by the pony during Christmastime. Macaroni was absolutely no relation to the feather in Yankee Doodle's hat!

Did You Know That . . .

★ John F. Kennedy was the first and only Roman Catholic president?

★ JFK was the youngest *elected* president? (Teddy Roosevelt, the youngest president, assumed office after McKinley was assassinated.)

★ Kennedy was one of two presidents buried at Arlington National Cemetery?

★ JFK was the first president born in the twentieth century?

★ John Kennedy won the Pulitzer Prize for writing *Profiles in Courage*? (The first and only president to do so.)

★ Kennedy was the only president to appoint his brother to a cabinet position? (Attorney general—Robert Kennedy.)

★ President Kennedy commissioned Pierre Salinger to buy and store over 1,500 H. Upmann Petit Corona cigars from Havana, Cuba, before signing the Cuban trade embargo?

★ Kennedy wore corrective shoes because his right leg was three-quarters of an inch longer than his left leg?

★ President Kennedy was the first president who had served in the U.S. Navy?

★ Kennedy suffered from chronic back pain his entire adult life from an injury he got in the navy?

★ President and Mrs. Kennedy lost two children, a daughter who was stillborn and a son who died when he was two days old?

★ Kennedy was the first president to win the Purple Heart?

★ JFK was the fourth U.S. president to be assassinated?

★ Kennedy loved Italian food?

★ John Kennedy was the first Boy Scout to become president?

★ Kennedy was the very first president to visit the pope during his term?

★ John Kennedy did not accept his presidential salary?

★ Kennedy donated his presidential salary to the United Negro College Fund, Jewish organizations, the Girl Scouts, and the Boy Scouts?

★ President Kennedy started the Peace Corps?

★ First Lady Jacqueline Kennedy began the effort to preserve the White House, with its portraits and furnishings, as a landmark in U.S. history?

★ JFK used this slogan when campaigning against Richard Nixon: "Would you buy a used car from this man?"

★ Kennedy was the first president to have his parents live longer than he did?

★ JFK talked to his dad by phone every day that he was president?

★ Kennedy swam in the White House pool daily for back therapy?

★ President Kennedy was allergic to most animal fur but that did not stop his family from having a menagerie of pets: dogs, a cat, a rabbit, ponies, hamsters, and birds?

★ First Lady Jacqueline Kennedy had all the television sets in the White House removed?

★ Jackie Kennedy, Caroline's mom, had one television brought back into the White House so that Caroline could watch *Lassie*?

★ President Kennedy never carried cash and as a result had to borrow from agents, friends, and family all the time?

★ Kennedy was an avid reader who could read up to 2,000 words per minute with 100 percent comprehension?

★ Alan Seeger's poem "I Have a Rendezvous with Death" was one of Kennedy's favorites?

★ Kennedy preferred two boiled eggs for breakfast each morning?

★ Thirty-two thousand people marched in Kennedy's inauguration parade?

★ President Kennedy's favorite room in the White House was the Green Room?

★ John F. Kennedy was the youngest president to die in office?

★ Joseph Kennedy, JFK's father, gave each of his nine children $1 million on their twenty-first birthday?

★ JFK participated in the very first televised presidential debates?

★ Kennedy had a bad attendance record when serving in Congress? (Health issues.)

★ During Kennedy's life he was given last rites four different times?

★ First Lady Jacqueline Kennedy had the White House completely remodeled and had the finished result televised?

★ Martin Luther King Jr. gave his "I Have a Dream" speech during Kennedy's administration?

★ President Kennedy was assassinated in Dallas, Texas, on November 22, 1963?

★ Lee Harvey Oswald is believed to be JFK's assassin, but there are also theories about the involvement of others?

★ JFK wore custom-made European suits?

★ Jackie Kennedy hired French chefs who cooked the president mainly bland food because he had stomach trouble?

★ The Kennedys had separate bedrooms in the White House?

★ First Lady Jacqueline Kennedy had a nursery made in the White House so that the children could play with friends their age?

★ The Kennedys had a dog named Pushinka that was given to them as a gift by Soviet leader Nikita Khrushchev?

★ JFK liked to read his children bedtime stories when he had time? (His favorites: "Snow White" and "Goldilocks and the Three Bears.")

★ Jackie Kennedy's favorite First Lady of all time was Bess Truman?

★ John F. Kennedy's golf scores were in the high seventies?

★ The National Cultural Center in Washington, D.C., was renamed to honor President Kennedy? (John F. Kennedy Center for the Performing Arts.)

★ Kennedy's senior thesis at Harvard University became a best-selling book called *Why England Slept*?

★ Kennedy was six feet tall and weighed about 170 pounds when he died?

★ President Kennedy loved sailing, swimming, golf, and touch football?

★ ★ ★ ★ ★ ★ ★ ★ ★ ★ ★ ★ ★ ★ ★ ★

Presidential Potpourri

The president has his own seal. It is the official seal of the office.

- The front of the seal contains an eagle with an olive branch in its left claw.

- The right claw holds a bundle of arrows.

- The olive branch symbolizes that America is a peaceful country.

- The arrows show that if needed, America will fight for what it believes in.

- The seal is on the back of the $1 bill.

BIRTHDAY: August 27, 1908,
in Stonewall, Texas

PARENTS: Samuel Ealy and Rebekah Baines Johnson

FIRST LADY: Claudia Alta ("Lady Bird") Taylor

KIDS: Lynda Bird and Luci Baines Johnson

COLLEGES: Southwest Texas State Teachers College;
Georgetown University Law School

JOBS BEFORE PRESIDENT: Teacher, Rancher,
Congressional Secretary, Congressman,
Naval Reserve Officer, U.S. Senator,
Vice President under John F. Kennedy

POLITICAL PARTY: Democratic

RELIGION: Disciples of Christ

AGE AT INAUGURATION: Fifty-five

YEARS IN OFFICE: 1963–1969

NICKNAMES: LBJ; Big Daddy

DIED: January 22, 1973

Lyndon Baines Johnson

#36

—had an ego the size of the state he came from. Texas is a huge state. Everything and everyone, including his staff, his family, and the world, revolved around him. Johnson was king and America was his kingdom.

President Johnson loved talking on the telephone. He kept advised and informed through the telephone so much that he had one installed everywhere he could think of: bathrooms, cars, boats, planes, swimming pools. He also loved TV and radio. He walked around most of the time with a transistor radio and had three different television sets so that he could watch all three networks at the very same time.

Johnson made high demands of his staff. One demand was to be available any time of day for meetings. Sometimes these meetings were held when Johnson was in bed, and everyone would go into his room for the meeting. Johnson often swam nude in the White House pool and called meetings in the pool as well. Johnson even had staffers meeting with him as he took care of business in the bathroom (if you know what I mean). Johnson was a sort of king and I guess this served as his *throne* room from time to time.

Johnson was a bully who loved to shock people with his words and his actions. Speaking of shock value, Johnson loved to have guests at his ranch and shock or scare them half to death. Johnson's favorite toy at his ranch was his amphibious car. He would often take a guest of choice for the ride of his or her life. He would drive straight for the lake at speeds of up to 90 mph and shout that the brakes were shot. The car would drive right into the lake with Johnson laughing his head off. (He had a really big head!)

Did You Know That . . .

★ Lyndon Johnson was the only president to take the presidential oath of office on an airplane? (Air Force One at Dallas Love Field.)

★ Johnson was the only president to receive the oath of office from a woman?

★ The Johnson family all had the same initials, LBJ? (Lyndon Baines Johnson, Lady Bird Johnson, Lynda Bird Johnson, Luci Baines Johnson.)

★ President Johnson loved the soft drink Fresca so much that he had a soda fountain that dispensed it installed in the Oval Office?

★ President Johnson's favorite foods were canned peas and tapioca?

★ Johnson's pet beagles were named Him and Her?

★ Him's pawprints are on the cement walkway that leads to the White House press room?

★ When Lyndon and Lady Bird were married, Lady Bird's wedding ring cost $2.50 at Sears?

★ President Johnson liked to play golf but always kept his score a secret?

★ Johnson ran away from home at age fifteen?

★ Johnson served in World War II and was awarded the Silver Star by General MacArthur?

★ President Johnson was six feet three inches tall and weighed 210 pounds?

★ Johnson had no vice president until he was reelected to his own term in 1964?

★ Johnson would sometimes lift up his shirt and show people his surgical scars?

★ During Johnson's term the United States fought in the Vietnam War and the war in the Dominican Republic?

★ His famous campaign slogan was "All the Way with LBJ!"?

★ Johnson was the very first president to have his State of the Union Address broadcast on all major networks? (1967—NBC, CBS, and ABC.)

★ President Johnson created the act that helped poor people with money for food? (The Food Stamp Act.)

★ The Johnsons hosted the first cookout at the White House?

★ Johnson signed the famous Civil Rights Act on July 2, 1964?

★ President Johnson had to have an oversized bed made just for him because of his size and height?

★ LBJ had an explosive temper?

★ Johnson hated when any White House staff or cabinet members left lights on in the White House? (He would go around and turn them off.)

★ Sometimes during meetings Johnson would declare a swim break?

★ Johnson appointed the first African American to the Supreme Court?

★ The first Super Bowl game was played during Johnson's presidency?

★ Lady Bird Johnson began the Head Start Program?

★ President Johnson was an excellent dancer?

★ Johnson fired the same Secret Service agent thirteen times?

★ Lyndon Johnson proposed to Lady Bird two days after meeting her? (On their first date.)

★ Johnson smoked three packs of cigarettes a day before his heart attack?

★ LBJ once had a Texas barbecue on the roof of the White House?

⋆ Lyndon Johnson was the first president to appoint an African American cabinet member?

⋆ Johnson had a special shower installed in the White House that allowed water to spray from every direction?

⋆ Aboard Air Force One, LBJ would conduct press interviews while having foot massages and pedicures?

⋆ Johnson learned the alphabet at age two?

⋆ President Johnson enjoyed playing dominoes?

BIRTHDAY: January 9, 1913,
in Yorba Linda, California

PARENTS: Francis Anthony and
Hannah Milhous Nixon

FIRST LADY: Thelma Catherine ("Pat") Ryan

KIDS: Patricia ("Tricia") and Julie Nixon

COLLEGES: Whittier College;
Duke University Law School

JOBS BEFORE PRESIDENT: Lawyer,
U.S. Naval Officer, Congressman, U.S. Senator,
Vice President under Dwight D. Eisenhower

POLITICAL PARTY: Republican

RELIGION: Quaker

AGE AT INAUGURATION: Fifty-six

YEARS IN OFFICE: 1969–1974

NICKNAME: Tricky Dick

DIED: April 22, 1994

Richard Milhous Nixon

#37

—was an excellent bowler and poker player. He financed his first run for Congress with over $10,000 of winnings that he had earned while playing poker in the navy. Yes, he was a lieutenant commander in the navy during World War II; he served in the South Pacific. Nixon was also a fanatical football fan. During Super Bowl VI, President Nixon phoned the head coach of the Miami Dolphins to recommend a play. They actually tried it and it never worked!

Richard and Pat Nixon met at Whittier College auditioning for a play. Pat Nixon had been an extra in a Hollywood movie and wanted to continue acting. The future president was so amazed by her that he proposed to her the same day he met her. She didn't say yes right away and wanted to date other people. Nixon was so determined to be her husband that his protective role kicked in right away. He offered to drive her to and from dates with other boys. He would drive her to the date, wait in the car for her, and then drive her back to her dorm. After two years of this, Pat Nixon finally gave in and married him.

The Nixon family dog, Checkers, actually saved the future president's career once. As veep for Dwight D. Eisenhower, Nixon was accused of taking funds from secret donors. He was so angry about the accusation that he went on television to make a speech about his integrity as a politician. He told the American people that he had taken no money *but* that he had accepted a puppy from a man in Texas. His daughters loved the dog and named the black-and-white cocker spaniel Checkers. Nixon told all of America that he was guilty only of taking Checkers and that he would not give him back no matter what.

Accusations and scandal continued to follow Nixon throughout his political career. Not even Checkers could help him out of Watergate.

Did You Know That . . .

★ Richard Nixon was the first president to visit China while in office?

★ Nixon's mom wanted him to be a Quaker missionary?

★ President Nixon had always wanted to be an FBI agent?

★ President Nixon suffered from motion sickness?

★ President Nixon's secretary of state won a Nobel Peace Prize? (Henry Kissinger.)

★ Nixon was the first president to address the Russians on Russian TV?

* Richard Nixon was the first president to visit all fifty states?

* Milhous was President Nixon's mother's maiden name and his middle name?

* Richard Nixon was the only president ever to resign from office?

* Nixon had the White House swimming pool filled in so that there would be more standing room for the press?

* Nixon was distantly related to William Taft and Herbert Hoover?

* Richard Nixon was one of two presidents who were Quakers? (The other was Hoover.)

* President Nixon was the first chief executive to speak to astronauts on the moon from the White House? (Via radiotelephone.)

* Nixon was the first president to attend a regular-season NFL game during his administration?

* Sometimes Nixon had a fire going in the fireplace and also had the air conditioner on?

* Nixon got involved in politics by answering an ad in a California newspaper?

* During Nixon's administration the Twenty-sixth Amendment to the Constitution was ratified, changing the voting age from twenty-one to eighteen?

* When Nixon became president, there had just been a pay increase from $100,000 to $200,000 per year?

* President Nixon shaved several times a day?

★ Tricia Nixon, President Nixon's daughter, was the first person to marry outdoors on the White House grounds? (In the Rose Garden.)

★ One of Nixon's favorite foods was meat loaf?

★ Nixon was a pianist?

★ Nixon had above-average scores in golf and bowling?

★ Nixon's reelection committee was known by the acronym CREEP? (Committee to Re-elect the President.)

★ President Nixon stopped the U.S. involvement in the Vietnam War?

★ The Nixons' younger daughter, Julie, married David Eisenhower? (The grandson of Dwight D. Eisenhower.)

★ Pat Nixon traveled to eighty-three foreign countries while she was First Lady?

★ When Richard Nixon was growing up, his family owned a store called Nixon's Market?

★ Nixon became a millionaire from his earnings as an author and a lawyer?

★ The first video game was invented during Nixon's administration? (*Pong.*)

★ Richard Nixon presented former president Harry Truman with a Steinway piano for display at his Presidential Library?

★ Nixon loved Elvis Presley music?

★ Elvis Presley once brought a handgun into the White House as a gift to Nixon?

★ Richard Nixon's face appeared on the cover of *Time* magazine a record fifty-six times?

★ President Nixon was five feet eleven and a half inches tall and weighed about 175 pounds?

★ President Nixon played golf? (His score was in the low nineties.)

★ In retirement Nixon mediated a contract dispute between Major League Baseball and the Major League Umpires Association? (1985.)

★ When he was retired, Nixon talked on the phone often to members of the Reagan administration? (Rarely with President Reagan.)

BIRTHDAY: July 14, 1913, in Omaha, Nebraska

PARENTS: Leslie Lynch King and
Dorothy Ayer Gardner King Ford
Stepfather: Gerald Rudolph Ford

FIRST LADY: Elizabeth Ann Bloomer ("Betty") Warren

KIDS: Michael Gerald, John Gardner ("Jack"),
Steven Meigs, and Susan Elizabeth Ford

COLLEGES: University of Michigan;
Yale Law School

JOBS BEFORE PRESIDENT: U.S. Naval Officer,
Lawyer, Congressman, Vice President
under Richard M. Nixon

POLITICAL PARTY: Republican

RELIGION: Episcopalian

AGE AT INAUGURATION: Sixty-one

YEARS IN OFFICE: 1974–1977

NICKNAME: Jerry

Gerald R. Ford

#38

—had political dreams of being the Speaker of the House. This was his ambition before he became veep for Richard Nixon. His path to politics started on the football fields of the University of Michigan. Ford was an extremely talented athlete with a promising career in professional football waiting for him. When Ford became president, he asked that the Marine Band play the University of Michigan fight song instead of "Hail to the Chief" at functions that involved his entering to music. A true football fan! Voted "Most Valuable Player" of the University of Michigan football team, he received offers to play pro ball for the Detroit Lions and the Green Bay Packers. Ford chose to go to law school at Yale instead.

The funny thing is that Gerald Ford wasn't Gerald Ford at all. Actually, he was born Leslie Lynch King Jr. He was named after his father. His parents divorced when he was very young. His mom married Gerald R. Ford when the future president was two years old. Ford legally adopted the baby. They began calling the baby Gerald R. Ford Jr. Later his name was legally changed from Leslie Lynch King Jr. to Gerald Rudolph Ford Jr. He would be the only King to become a U.S. president.

President and Mrs. Ford were both models before becoming political leaders. Ford had been on the covers of several popular magazines and Mrs. Ford was a professional dancer and model. Even though President Ford was athletic, he was constantly falling down and bumping into things and wasn't too sure on his own two feet. Besides not being sure-footed, he wasn't too sure of his shoe choice, either. When he proposed to Betty, he was wearing one brown shoe and one black one. I guess his motto was "If the shoe fits . . . go ahead and wear it, even if it doesn't match your other one."

Did You Know That . . .

★ Ford always signed his formal signature "Jerry Ford"?

★ Ford was the only man who served as vice president and president without ever being elected? (He was appointed V.P. when Spiro Agnew resigned.)

★ Ford was running for Congress and campaigned on his actual wedding day?

★ Gerald Ford was the first president to pardon a former president?

★ Ford was once locked out of the White House when walking his dog, Liberty? (The Secret Service let him back in.)

★ Ford was the first president to be an Eagle Scout?

★ The Fords' daughter, Susan, held her senior prom at the White House?

★ Gerald Ford was the first president to visit Japan?

★ Ford was the second chief executive to make a hole in one while playing golf?

★ Gerald Ford was a member of the Warren Commission, which investigated JFK's assassination?

★ Ford was the only president who was born in Nebraska?

★ Ford was a decorated naval officer during World War II?

★ Gerald Ford almost died when serving in World War II with the Third Fleet in the South Pacific? (A typhoon struck, killing 800 men.)

★ President Ford loved to eat cottage cheese with ketchup?

★ When Ford first became president, he toasted his own English muffin each morning?

★ Betty Ford had danced with the famous Martha Graham Dance Company?

★ Ford graduated in the top third of his class at Yale?

★ President Ford rode an exercise bike and lifted weights in the White House?

★ After leaving the White House, First Lady Betty Ford founded the Betty Ford Center, which helps people with drug and alcohol addictions?

* America turned 200 when Gerald Ford was president?

* President Ford's favorite dessert at the White House was butter pecan ice cream?

* Ford redesigned the official coat of arms, the U.S. seal, and the flag of the vice president? (These are still in use now.)

* Ford was awarded the Presidential Medal of Freedom by President Clinton for his efforts to forgive and move on after the Watergate scandal?

* Betty Ford was awarded the Presidential Medal of Freedom by President George H. W. Bush for her drug and alcohol rehabilitation efforts?

* President Ford hired a professional joke writer?

* President Ford sometimes had help from his dog, Liberty, when Oval Office meetings went too long? (The dog would break into the meeting.)

* Ford was right-handed when throwing a ball and left-handed when writing and eating?

* President Ford asked all of his Secret Service agents to smile more often?

* Ford smoked a pipe each day?

* First Lady Betty Ford publicized her own fight with breast cancer to raise awareness?

* The Vietnam War officially ended during Ford's presidency? (Nixon had ended U.S. involvement during his administration.)

★ The *Viking* spacecraft landed on Mars during Ford's presidency?

★ Steven Ford, the Fords' son, was an actor on the soap opera *The Young and the Restless*?

★ Ford was six feet tall and weighed 195 pounds as president?

BIRTHDAY: October 1, 1924,
in Plains, Georgia

PARENTS: James Earl and Lillian Gordy Carter

FIRST LADY: Eleanor Rosalynn Smith

KIDS: John William ("Jack"), James Earl ("Chip"),
Donnel Jeffrey ("Jeff"), and Amy Lynn Carter

COLLEGE: U.S. Naval Academy

JOBS BEFORE PRESIDENT: U.S. Naval Officer,
Farmer, Georgia State Senator, Governor of Georgia

POLITICAL PARTY: Democratic

RELIGION: Baptist

AGE AT INAUGURATION: Fifty-two

YEARS IN OFFICE: 1977–1981

NICKNAME: Jimmy

Jimmy Carter
#39

—graduated 59th out of his 820 graduating classmates from Annapolis. He majored in nuclear physics in the Naval Academy's submarine program. His intellect was amazing and he was also a speed-reader at 2,000 words per minute with 95 percent accuracy. It is hard to imagine that this intellectual giant was raised on a peanut farm with no electricity or indoor plumbing. However, he *was* the first president to be born in a hospital.

A first for any president, this future one once wore women's shoes to high school. No, he wasn't trying to dress like a woman or act like one in any way. He had no weird habit or desire to be a woman. Relax, they were not high heels, either. Jimmy's dad, a local supply-store owner, had ordered a larger supply of women's high-buttoned shoes than he could possibly sell in one season. In order to be thrifty and practical, he passed out a pair to each child in the family. . . . Yes, even the future president got a pair.

Carter discussed his presidential decisions with his entire family. His three older sons, younger daughter, Amy, and wife, Rosalynn, were all known as "the family cabinet." They regularly made suggestions about important decisions that Jimmy had to make as president and shared their opinions about how he should handle things. Amy Carter was nine when her dad became president and she attended a nearby Washington, D.C., public school. Amy had her own tree house built on the White House grounds and played in it with friends. Once, when she had a school project that required her to label the trees around the White House, her dad thought it was such a great idea that he had each tree labeled with its common and Latin names as well as information like its age, its donor, and who planted it.

We have all heard the song "Here comes Peter Cottontail, hopping down the bunny trail. . . ." This causes thoughts of cute little fluffy white Easter bunnies. President Jimmy Carter was once attacked by a huge rabbit and it wasn't one of those cute little fluffy Easter ones, either. He was fishing in a pond on his Georgia farm when a huge, mad, burly "swamp thing" of a rabbit tried to climb aboard his boat. The animal was enraged and making strange hissing noises as well as showing its teeth while it was making its way aboard the fishing boat. President Carter slapped at the woolly thing with the boat paddle and the *thing* eventually swam away. Could you use the adage here never to trust a wolf in rabbit's clothing?

Did You Know That . . .

★ In 1953 Carter returned to his family peanut farm in Georgia to take over daily operations?

★ Jimmy Carter improved production on the farm and became a millionaire in the peanut industry?

★ Carter was once on a game show called *What's My Line*?

★ President Carter was the first president to be sworn into office using his nickname?

★ President Carter conducted the very first presidential phone-in? (Over 9 million people tried to call.)

★ Carter played basketball in high school?

★ Jimmy Carter was the only president from Georgia?

★ Carter was distantly related to Elvis Presley?

★ The parade at Carter's inauguration had a giant peanut balloon in it?

★ The Carter family dog was named Grits?

★ Carter established that human rights would be the focus of his foreign policy?

★ Carter read three to four books every week?

★ President Carter pardoned all draft dodgers during his administration?

★ Carter was known to have had a red "lucky" tie?

★ During her husband's administration, First Lady Rosalynn Carter devoted herself to the problem of mental illness?

★ Carter worked to create a way for those in need to have homes through a group called Habitat for Humanity? (After his presidency.)

★ Billy beer was named for President Carter's brother, Billy?

★ Jimmy Carter was the very first president to walk the inaugural route all the way from the Capitol to the White House?

★ One of Carter's fingers was permanently bent because of a cotton gin accident?

★ President Carter had classical music piped into his Oval Office?

★ President Carter taught Sunday school at the First Baptist Church of Washington, D.C.?

★ President Carter's nickname as a child was Hot Shot?

★ Carter was the first candidate from the Deep South to be elected president since the Civil War?

★ Carter once reported seeing a UFO?

★ President Carter was awarded the Nobel Peace Prize in 2002? (He was one of three presidents to receive it.)

★ President Carter negotiated a peace treaty between Egypt and Israel?

★ First Lady Rosalynn Carter attended many cabinet meetings with her husband?

★ President Carter used Bible passage Micah 6:8 in his inaugural address?

★ President Carter gave control of the Panama Canal back to Panama?

★ Carter called for a boycott of the 1980 Summer Olympics?

★ The Apple II personal computer was first marketed during Carter's presidency?

★ The first test-tube baby was born during Carter's administration?

★ Carter had all the White House thermostats turned down to save energy?

★ Carter wore casual clothes with old cardigan sweaters around the White House?

★ The Carters liked watching movies together? (They watched over 465 movies during his presidency.)

★ Amy's cat was named Misty Malarky Ying Yang?

★ The Carters' cat became an enemy of Grits the dog?

★ President Carter was five feet nine and a half inches tall and weighed 155 pounds as president?

★ Jimmy Carter is the most effective and active former president ever?

★ Former president Carter and his wife have been and continue to be activists for peace and the homeless, special diplomats, authors, artists, home builders, Sunday school teachers, and active community members?

★ The Carters still take their turn once a month teaching Sunday school and cleaning the churchyard at their church in Plains, Georgia?

★ Jimmy Carter planned at age twelve to go to the U.S. Naval Academy and began to solicit people to write letters of recommendation for him?

★ Carter was fearful that being flat-footed would keep him from getting into Annapolis, so he rolled his feet back and forth on Coke bottles and stood on them to strengthen his arches?

BIRTHDAY: February 6, 1911,
in Tampico, Illinois

PARENTS: John Edward and Nelle Wilson Reagan

FIRST LADY: Nancy Davis

KIDS: Maureen Elizabeth, Michael Edward (adopted),
Patricia Ann, and Ronald Prescott Reagan

COLLEGE: Eureka College

JOBS BEFORE PRESIDENT:
Radio Sports Commentator, Actor, U.S. Army Officer,
Rancher, Governor of California

POLITICAL PARTY: Republican

RELIGION: Disciples of Christ

AGE AT INAUGURATION: Sixty-nine

YEARS IN OFFICE: 1981–1989

NICKNAMES: The Gipper; Ronnie;
Dutch; the Great Communicator

DIED: June 5, 2004

Ronald Wilson Reagan

#40

—was known as the Great Communicator. However, there is a lot of evidence that he was also the Great Jelly Bean Eater. Yes, the fortieth leader of the free world was addicted to jelly beans. When Reagan first became the governor of the great state of California, he began to spill the beans—all over his desk, that is—and then proceeded to eat them. He was trying to give up pipe smoking, and the jelly beans helped him kick the habit.

Three and a half tons of Jelly Belly jelly beans were shipped to the White House for Reagan's 1981 presidential inauguration. The blueberry-flavored blue jelly bean was designed specifically for the new president, in keeping with the patriotic theme of red, white, and blue. After the inauguration was over and for the next eight years you could always find a jar of assorted gourmet Jelly

Belly jelly beans in the Oval Office and the Cabinet Room of the White House. It seemed that Reagan's cabinet and White House staff were also addicted.

If you visit the Ronald Reagan Presidential Library and Museum in Simi Valley, California, you will find a portrait of the fortieth president of the United States in, you guessed it, Jelly Belly jelly beans. Actually the portrait is of a smiling Ronald Reagan made with over 10,000 jelly beans. There is some controversy out there about what flavor was the Gipper's favorite. Conflicting sources report coconut, licorice, and blueberry. . . . Perhaps we will never know.

Jelly Belly jelly beans were even served aboard Air Force One. Special containers were designed so that turbulence would not "spill the beans" all over those enjoying them.

Did You Know That . . .

★ Ronald Reagan was the oldest president in history?

★ President Reagan was the very first president to be divorced?

★ President Reagan was the only president to have been wounded by a would-be assassin and survived?

★ Reagan was the only president to have been the head of a labor union?

★ Reagan and Nancy Davis appeared in a Hollywood movie together? (*Hellcats of the Navy.*)

★ President Reagan transferred presidential powers to Vice President George H. W. Bush while he had surgery for cancer?

★ Even though Reagan was a Republican, his model for the presidency was Franklin Roosevelt?

★ Ronald Reagan was the first president to have worn a hearing aid?

★ Reagan was the only president to have been an actor?

★ Ronald Reagan was the first president to wear contact lenses?

★ Hearing aid sales went up by 40 percent when America found out their president wore one?

★ Reagan once broke his leg in six different places when he flew into first base at a celebrity baseball game?

★ Reagan loved horseback riding?

★ Right after being shot President Reagan joked, "I forgot to duck"?

★ Reagan liked to read newspapers and turned to the comic pages first?

★ Reagan acted in over fifty movies?

★ Ronald Reagan celebrated his seventieth birthday seventeen days after his inauguration?

★ First Lady Nancy Reagan started the campaign against drugs called "Just Say No"?

★ Nancy Reagan tasted all the food that White House guests would be served?

★ Reagan wore, and all presidents after him now wear, bulletproof vests?

★ The space shuttle *Challenger* exploded right after takeoff during Reagan's presidency?

★ Ronald Reagan appointed the very first female Supreme Court justice, Sandra Day O'Connor?

★ A gun fired during a movie shoot left Reagan almost deaf in one ear?

★ Reagan and his wife both earned the Congressional Medal of Honor?

★ President Reagan's favorite place to retreat was his California ranch, Rancho del Cielo?

★ Reagan once hosted two famous TV shows, *The General Electric Theater* and *Death Valley Days*?

★ Ronald Reagan changed from a Democrat to a Republican in 1952?

★ Ronald Reagan is often referred to as the president with the most optimistic personality?

★ John Hinckley Jr. tried to assassinate President Reagan?

★ Reagan had a daughter and an adopted son with his first wife and a daughter and a son with Nancy?

★ At 5 P.M. each day President Reagan would put on swim trunks and go swim and work out?

★ The Reagans loved Mexican food?

★ The Reagans liked to watch TV while eating their supper on TV trays?

★ Nancy Reagan consulted an astrologer after her husband had been shot so that his schedule could be arranged around the days that were safer than others?

★ Reagan's favorite song was "Battle Hymn of the Republic"?

★ Ron Reagan, President Reagan's son, was a ballet dancer and a journalist?

★ Patti, the Reagans' daughter, was an actress and a writer?

★ Nancy Reagan wrote several books?

★ Reagan built up the army, navy, and air force when he was president?

★ As a young lifeguard Reagan once received a $10 tip for diving into a river and finding a lost set of false teeth?

★ The Reagans' dog, Rex, was given a doghouse from the Washington Children's Museum?

★ Rex's doghouse had a shingled roof, red curtains, and framed portraits of the president and First Lady?

★ Ronald Reagan loved earlobes?

★ Ronald Reagan collected bird eggs and butterflies as a kid?

★ Reagan was the first U.S. president to address a joint session of the British Parliament?

★ Ronald Reagan shared his diagnosis of Alzheimer's disease with America?

★ Reagan was six feet one inch tall and weighed around 185 pounds?

BIRTHDAY: June 12, 1924,
in Milton, Massachusetts

PARENTS: Prescott Sheldon
and Dorothy Walker Bush

FIRST LADY: Barbara Pierce

KIDS: George Walker, Pauline Robinson
("Robin") (1949–1953), John Ellis ("Jeb"),
Neil Mallon, Marvin Pierce, and Dorothy Walker Bush

COLLEGE: Yale

JOBS BEFORE PRESIDENT: U.S. Naval Pilot, Oilman,
Congressman, U.S. Ambassador to United Nations,
CIA Director, Vice President under Ronald Reagan

POLITICAL PARTY: Republican

RELIGION: Episcopalian

AGE AT INAUGURATION: Sixty-four

YEARS IN OFFICE: 1989–1993

NICKNAME: Poppy

George H. W. Bush

#41

—is most likely the best foreign policy president that the United States has ever known! His political résumé is long and distinguished, and he was the first president to have headed the CIA! He was a two-term congressman and a U.N. ambassador, not to mention vice president for eight years. George H. W. Bush was the first sitting vice president since Martin Van Buren in 1836 to be elected president.

George Bush is a hero, not just for being a chief executive, but for being a brave nineteen-year-old who was a fearless TBM Avenger aviator in the Pacific during World War II. He was the youngest pilot in the navy's history. His plane was shot down into an ocean that was infested with hungry sharks. With a head injury and the loss of his crew members, he waited for over three hours to be rescued while being snacked on by Portuguese men-of-war. He concentrated on the fact that he was alive and focused his thoughts on his family.

Not many presidents can be credited with creating new words for the Japanese dictionary. President Bush did! In January 1992, Bush was in Tokyo, Japan, attending a state dinner. He was seated next to Japanese prime minister Kiichi Miyazawa. Suddenly President Bush became pale and sick. He proceeded to throw up all over the prime minister and then pass out. This incident was responsible for a new Japanese slang word in their dictionary that is still in use today: the verb *Bushusuru* (literally, "Bushing it") to refer to puking or vomiting. He couldn't even blame broccoli; he just had the flu.

Did You Know That . . .

★ George H. W. Bush played first base for the Yale baseball team? (He was captain.)

★ President Bush is distantly related to Benedict Arnold, Marilyn Monroe, Franklin Pierce, Abraham Lincoln, Teddy Roosevelt, Gerald Ford, and Winston Churchill?

★ Bush flew fifty-eight combat missions?

★ Bush is left-handed?

★ George H. W. Bush was the first president to be born in June?

★ President Bush loved to fish, especially on his boat?

★ Bush was one of four presidents from Massachusetts?

★ Even though Bush was born in Massachusetts, he considered Texas his home state?

★ The Bush family had a springer spaniel named Millie?

★ Millie had her own room (the former beauty parlor of Nancy Reagan)?

★ Bush's favorite game was horseshoes?

★ Bush was the only president to have parachuted out of an airplane? (Once in World War II [1944] and in 1997 and 2004.)

★ Bush was a member of the Skull and Bones Club at Yale?

★ Bush's father was a senator from Connecticut?

★ George H. W. Bush loved to snack on pork rinds doused with Tabasco sauce?

★ First Lady Barbara Bush promoted literacy while in the White House?

★ George and Barbara's daughter Robin died at age three of leukemia?

★ George and Barbara met at a school dance?

★ George H. W. Bush was the second president to have a son become president? (The other was John Adams.)

★ George H. W. Bush was the first president to be rescued by a submarine? (In World War II.)

★ The Bushes' dog, Millie, authored a book (with help from Barbara) that raised millions of dollars for Barbara Bush's reading programs?

★ Bush made his money as a Texas oilman?

★ Barbara Bush hung her famous gingerbread-man cookies on the White House Christmas tree?

★ When guests came to visit the president and First Lady during the Christmas holidays, the First Couple would give them gingerbread men right off the tree in little bags as mementos to take home with them?

★ George H. W. Bush is six feet two inches tall and weighed 195 pounds during his presidency?

★ Bush is a huge Houston Astros fan?

★ Bush was distantly related to his own vice president? (He is a tenth cousin once removed of Dan Quayle.)

★ In retirement Bush oversees programs at his library and jumps out of airplanes?

★ ★ ★ ★ ★ ★ ★ ★ ★ ★ ★ ★ ★ ★ ★ ★

The Secret Service

Began operation on July 5, 1865, in Washington, D.C.

★

Its original role was to suppress counterfeit currency.

★

In 1894 the Secret Service began protecting
President Grover Cleveland.

★

In 1902 the Secret Service assumed full responsibility
in the protection of the U.S. president.

★

In 1917 Congress authorized protection of
the U.S. president's immediate family.

★

In 1961 Congress authorized protection of
all former U.S. presidents.

BIRTHDAY: August 19, 1946,
in Hope, Arkansas

PARENTS: William Jefferson Blythe III and
Virginia Dell Cassidy Blythe Clinton Dwire Kelley
Stepfather: Roger Clinton

FIRST LADY: Hillary Diane Rodham

KID: Chelsea Victoria Clinton

COLLEGES: Georgetown University;
Oxford University; Yale Law School

JOBS BEFORE PRESIDENT: Lawyer, Law Professor,
Arkansas Attorney General, Governor of Arkansas

POLITICAL PARTY: Democratic

RELIGION: Baptist

AGE AT INAUGURATION: Forty-six

YEARS IN OFFICE: 1993–2001

NICKNAMES: Slick Willy; Bill; Bubba; Comeback Kid

Bill Clinton

#42

—was born William Jefferson Blythe IV. He was named after his father, William Jefferson Blythe III, who was killed in a car accident three months before the future president was born. When he was a toddler, his grandparents became his guardians because his mom was going to nursing school in New Orleans. His grandparents were grocery store merchants in a poor section of Hope, Arkansas. They taught "Billy" how to count and read by age three. He loved his grandparents and learned from them tolerance and acceptance of all people. His mom married Roger Clinton and they moved to Hot Springs, Arkansas. They had a son, Roger, who is Clinton's only sibling.

Clinton says one of his earliest memories was a traumatic one. He was attacked by a sheep. (This is a baaaahhhd memory.)

When Clinton was seven or eight, a sheep began chasing him, and he says that he was too young, chubby, and slow to get away. The ram butted him and cut his head open. The ram butted him a second time and knocked him to the ground. Clinton remembers at least ten butts (and he is not referring to any of those in power in the Republican Congress). He refers to this as his worst beating and recalls that he was taken to the hospital for stitches.

Clinton was an excellent musician who loved everything from Elvis Presley to Bach. He played tenor and alto saxophone. Clinton and two friends formed a jazz trio. Clinton played sax, and his two friends played piano and drums. The group always performed wearing sunglasses, earning them the name Three Blind Mice. This president took office declaring, "I never inhaled." I guess he wasn't talking about playing the saxophone.

Did You Know That . . .

★ Bill Clinton is left-handed?

★ President Clinton had a dog named Buddy and a cat named Socks?

★ Clinton is allergic to cats?

★ Clinton was the only president to be elected twice without ever receiving 50 percent of the popular vote?

★ Bill Clinton was the only left-handed president to serve two terms?

★ President Clinton's favorite foods were peanut butter and banana sandwiches, tacos, and mango ice cream? (Cheeseburgers, too.)

★ President Clinton suffered from chronic laryngitis?

★ Bill Clinton's nickname growing up was Bubba?

★ Clinton met President John F. Kennedy when he was seventeen?

★ Bill Clinton was the second president to be impeached? (The first was Andrew Johnson.)

★ President Clinton added storytelling by celebrities to the annual Easter Egg Roll?

★ Hillary Clinton was the first First Lady to seek and win elected office?

★ Mrs. Clinton was the first First Lady to be a lawyer?

★ Clinton was the first president to be sued and forced to give a deposition while in office?

★ President Clinton was six feet two and a half inches tall and weighed between 215 and 243 pounds during his administration?

★ President Clinton has collected books about the lives of the presidents since he was a kid?

★ President Clinton liked to jog every morning?

★ Clinton enjoyed golf while in office and still plays?

★ The Clintons sheltered and protected their only daughter, Chelsea, as she grew up in the White House?

★ President Clinton loved to play cards?

★ President Clinton liked to go shopping at malls?

★ Clinton demonstrated against the Vietnam War in the 1960s?

★ Bill Clinton was a Rhodes Scholar?

★ Clinton is said to have been our most intelligent president?

★ When Clinton was elected governor of Arkansas, he was the youngest governor in history?

★ Bill and Hillary met in law school?

★ Chelsea took ballet lessons while growing up in the White House?

★ Former president Clinton had heart bypass surgery in retirement?

★ Clinton formed a partnership with former president Bush for a tsunami relief fund and traveled to the ravaged area to offer encouragement and help?

★ Clinton left the note given to him his first day in office by President George H. W. Bush (41) for President George W. Bush (43) on his first day?

★ The Oklahoma City federal building was bombed during the Clinton presidency?

★ President Clinton loved to golf, swim, and play basketball?

★ Bill Clinton is a good hearts and pinochle player?

★ Clinton nominated Ruth Bader Ginsburg to the Supreme Court?

★ Former president Clinton's memoirs are considered best-selling? (Over 2 million copies.)

★ ★ ★ ★ ★ ★ ★ ★ ★ ★ ★ ★ ★ ★ ★ ★ ★

To Be the President . . .

- You must be a natural-born citizen of the United States. (In Colonial times you had to be either a natural-born citizen or a citizen at the time the Constitution was adopted.)

- You have to be at least thirty-five years of age.

- As a citizen you must have lived in the United States for at least fourteen years.

★

As President . . .

- You earn $400,000 per year.

- You live rent free in the White House.

- You have use of Air Force One, Army One, Coast Guard One, Executive One, Marine One, and Navy One.

- You have full use of Camp David in Maryland.

- You have your own oval-shaped office.

- You hold the highest, most powerful office in the world.

- You preside over the executive branch of government.

- You have more responsibility than anyone else in the world.

BIRTHDAY: July 6, 1946,
in New Haven, Connecticut

PARENTS: George Herbert Walker and
Barbara Pierce Bush

FIRST LADY: Laura Welch

KIDS: Barbara Pierce and Jenna Welch Bush
(fraternal twins)

COLLEGES: Yale; Harvard Business School

JOBS BEFORE PRESIDENT: Texas Air National
Guard Pilot, Oilman, Owner of Texas Rangers
Baseball Team, Governor of Texas

POLITICAL PARTY: Republican

RELIGION: Methodist

AGE AT INAUGURATION: Fifty-four

YEARS IN OFFICE: 2001–present

NICKNAMES: Dubya; Quincy; Junior; 43

George W. Bush

#43

—didn't dream as a young boy of someday being president. He dreamed instead of being Willie Mays! Yes, this president was and still is a baseball fanatic. He was taken out to the ball game (so to speak) a lot! As a toddler he watched his dad play baseball for Yale. He was catcher on a Little League team in Midland, Texas (the first Little Leaguer to become president). His uncle was part owner of the Mets and, of course, he went to watch the Mets play. He lived in Houston for a while and watched the Astros at the Astrodome. He pitched at Andover and played a year at Yale, then was on to his dream job of being an owner of the Texas Rangers. Cool!

As a kid it is said that George W. Bush had the finest card collection on the block. He was constantly looking for a pickup game to play instead of doing his homework. At a young age he could rattle off accurate statistics of all the professional baseball players (a skill he still has). His friends learned that young George was a savvy card collector and that a trade with him could mean gain for him and not for them. Bush to this day still dabbles in baseball memorabilia, owning a collection of over 250 autographed baseballs that would make even Babe Ruth green with envy.

When George W. Bush was managing partner of the Texas Rangers, he was given a luxury box, where he could view the games in style. He never sat in it. He preferred to be in the stands with the fans buying peanuts and Cracker Jack and cheering his team to victory. When he first saw *Field of Dreams,* Bush is said to have cried. He now keeps up with his Texas Rangers not from the stands but from the BottomBell service on his cell phone. This provides him with game updates and final game summaries on demand—the next best thing to being there.

He didn't get to be Willie Mays, but he did get to be the forty-third leader of the free world! When being interviewed after becoming president in 2001, Bush reported that his happiest memory of all time was playing catcher on the Little League team that his dad coached in Midland. . . . Hmmm.

Did You Know That . . .

* George W. earned a bachelor's degree from Yale and a master's degree from Harvard?

* George W. Bush was in the oil and gas business in Midland, Texas?

* Bush married Laura Welch and claims it is the best thing he ever did in his life?

★ President and Mrs. Bush's twin daughters are named after their grandmothers? (Barbara and Jenna.)

★ Bush is the only president to be born in Connecticut?

★ Bush is the president with the lowest heart rate?

★ George W. Bush is the first president who mountain bikes? (Up to fifteen miles a day on his ranch.)

★ President Bush loves peanut butter and jelly sandwiches?

★ Bush is the second son of a president to become president?

★ Bush is the only president to have a dog named Barney?

★ Laura Bush is the only First Lady to have delivered an entire presidential radio address?

★ Mrs. Bush is a former teacher and librarian?

★ George and Laura Bush attended the same junior high school?

★ George W. Bush was the first president to be elected in the twenty-first century?

★ The U.S. Supreme Court decided four weeks after the 2000 election that Bush was the winner?

★ President Bush choked on a pretzel while watching a football game on TV in the White House?

★ Bush raised over $36 million for his first presidential campaign?

★ President Bush added a new cabinet position, the secretary of homeland security?

★ Bush was the first president to select an African American secretary of state? (Colin Powell.)

★ George W. Bush once repaired his broken bed with neckties?

★ Bush drove his car into the wall of the garage when Laura was critical of a speech he had just made?

★ George W. was a cheerleader in high school?

★ George married Laura only three months after meeting her?

★ The Bushes have a longhorn cow named Ofelia?

★ Dick Cheney was Bush's father's secretary of defense?

★ The letter "W" was missing from all computer keyboards in the White House when Bush moved in after the Clintons moved out?

★ President Bush was a Cub Scout as a boy?

★ President Bush's main form of exercise is biking while listening to his iPod?

★ President Bush is six feet tall and weighs approximately 192 pounds?

★ George W. and Laura Bush are the first president and First Lady to have been the parents of fraternal twins?

★ President Bush's twin daughters gave him an iPod for his fifty-eighth birthday?

★ A lot of the songs on President Bush's iPod are country music by George Jones, Alan Jackson, and Kenny Chesney?

★ One of President Bush's favorite songs on his iPod is "Brown Eyed Girl" by Van Morrison?

★ George W. Bush is the only president to have an M.B.A. degree?

Noah's Ultimate Political Quiz

FIVE LEVELS OF POLITICAL SAVVY

GOOD LUCK!

Governor Level

1. What former king was a U.S. president?

2. What is the age requirement to run for U.S. president?

3. Which president loved baseball and started the tradition of presidents throwing out the "first pitch"?

4. Who was the only physically disabled president?

5. Which chief executive loved jelly beans?

6. What allergies does Bill Clinton have?

7. Which president once saved the lives of over seventy-eight people as a lifeguard?

8. Which president proposed to his future wife on their very first date?

9. Which three presidents had no religious affiliation?

10. Who was the only president born in California?

11. Have there been more Republican or Democratic presidents?

12. Which presidents were avid marble players?

13. Who was the first president to live in the White House?

14. Who was the first former U.S. senator to become president?

15. How old was Bill Clinton when he became the youngest governor in U.S. history?

16. Which four presidents were from the Whig Party?

17. Which chief executive kept a cow on the White House lawn so that he could have fresh milk?

18. How many words are in the presidential oath of office that each president must say before committing to lead the country?

19. Who was the tallest president?

20. Who was the heaviest president?

21. Who was the smallest president?

22. Who was the only president to have been a Hollywood actor?

23. Who was the first president to have a pilot's license?

24. Who was the first president born in a hospital?

25. Who was the youngest president?

26. Who was the oldest president?

27. Who was the only president never to be elected president or vice president?

28. How many presidents have died in office?

29. Name the presidents who were assassinated.

30. Name the presidents who survived assassination attempts.

U.S. House of Representatives Level

1. Which chief executive asked to be wrapped in the Stars and Stripes with a copy of the Constitution beneath his head when he died?

2. Which president predicted his death before he was assassinated?

3. Which president spoke four languages?

4. What wood is the Lincoln bed in the White House made of?

5. Which president added the first swimming pool to the White House?

6. Which presidents appear on U.S. coin currency?

7. Who was the first non-British subject to be president?

8. Which president invented the swivel chair?

9. On what currency do you see the White House?

10. Which former president was addicted to cocaine?

11. Which two U.S. presidents died on July 4, 1826?

12. What is the seating capacity of the State Dining Room in the White House?

13. How many presidents are not buried in the United States?

14. Who was one of President Carter's favorite presidents?

15. Which president liked to barbecue steaks on the roof of the White House?

16. What constitutional amendment was ratified in 1951 that changed the office of president forever?

17. Who appointed the first White House physician?

18. In which state were more presidents born than any other?

19. There are forty-two men who have been president. Why is George W. Bush number forty-three?

20. Who first used the term "First Lady"?

21. Which four presidents won the popular vote but lost the presidential election?

22. If something happens to the president and vice president, who is in charge?

23. Which four presidents lived past their ninetieth birthdays?

24. Which nine presidents are on U.S. paper currency?

25. Name the two presidents who actually died in the White House.

26. Which president died on July 4, 1831?

27. Who was the only president to be born on July 4?

28. Name the first vice president to take office due to the death of the president.

29. What was wrong with Abraham Lincoln when he gave the Gettysburg Address?

30. Which president and First Lady were both lawyers?

U.S. Senator Level

1. Who is the only president to have a foreign capital named after him?

2. How many presidents served in the military?

3. How many presidents were born in log cabins?

4. Name the two presidents who ran unopposed.

5. What is the current salary of the U.S. president?

6. Who was Gerald Ford's vice president?

7. Name the president who came up with the Maxwell House coffee slogan "Good to the Last Drop!"

8. Which president kept four different clocks on his Oval Office desk?

9. Which chief executive installed a bowling lane in the White House?

10. How long had President Kennedy been married when he died?

11. Which president did Gerald Ford have a bust of in his Oval Office?

12. Who was the only twentieth-century president never to go to college?

13. Which sign did Ronald Reagan have on his Oval Office desk?

     a. *It Can Be Done*
     b. *The Buck Stops Here*

14. What did Richard Nixon do to FDR's swimming pool at the White House?

15. Which U.S. president was a twin?

16. Who was the first president to take his oath of office inside the White House?

17. Which president born in Connecticut became a two-term governor of Texas?

18. What is the acreage of the White House grounds?

19. When was the West Wing added to the White House?

20. Name the first president to win a Nobel Peace Prize.

21. What did outgoing president Adams do to anger president-elect Jefferson?

22. What is the largest room in the White House?

23. Where does the vice president live?

24. Who was the first president sworn into office by a woman?

25. Which president was the first Little League baseball player to become president?

26. Which First Lady broke with tradition and became the first to have her office located in the West Wing?

27. Which president had written a Pulitzer Prize–winning book before taking office?

28. Which chief executive lived across the street from the White House for most of his second term?

29. Which president had a wife named Martha whose last name was not Washington?

30. Which First Lady was fluent in five different languages?

Vice President Level

1. Name the seven left-handed presidents.

2. List the first five office-holders in the presidential succession line.

3. How long is the official inaugural parade route?

4. How many bathrooms are in the White House?

5. Who was the only president to have an asteroid named after him?

6. Name the architect who designed the White House.

7. Who was the only president to have twins?

8. Who was the first president to have been a judge?

9. Name the first chief executive to fly in an airplane while in office.

10. Which president hosted his daughter's senior prom at the White House?

11. Which presidents were accomplished pianists?

12. Which president appointed the first female cabinet member?

13. How many presidents had the first name James?

14. What was Harry Truman's shoe size?

15. Did Jimmy Carter work for FDR?

16. Name the hour and day the White House gets a new First Family.

17. From which room in the White House did Nixon televise his resignation speech?

18. What presidential pet is buried next to her chief executive master?

19. Which president left the White House each and every Sunday with a sealed envelope? What was in the envelope?

20. Who was the youngest elected president?

21. Why did George H. W. Bush have to keep away from his family for several days?

22. Name the woman in a framed picture on Calvin Coolidge's desk when he was governor, vice president, and president.

23. Who was the only vice president to be elected to the office of president since Martin Van Buren?

24. Who was the only president to have divorced?

25. Which incumbent vice presidents won election to the presidency?

26. What group had President Reagan just given a speech to at the Washington Hilton when he was shot?

27. Which president allowed no visitors to the White House on Sundays?

28. Which signers of the Declaration of Independence became presidents?

29. Why was the official inaugural date changed from March 4 to January 20?

30. Which president always read the comic section of the newspaper first?

"Hail to the Chief" Level

1. Whom did Nixon defeat in the 1972 election?

2. Which president read the entire Bible every year?

3. Which of the last ten presidents did not play golf?

4. Which two presidents were born in the same city on the same street?

5. Which president slept more than ten hours each night and took an afternoon nap every day?

6. What kind of Cuban cigars did John F. Kennedy love?

7. Which U.S. government officials are not allowed to travel together?

8. Who lit the eternal flame at JFK's grave?

9. How close was the popular vote in the election of 1960 between JFK and Richard Nixon?

10. Which future presidents were elected to Congress in 1946?

11. Who was the first union president to become U.S. president?

12. Which president added seven rooms to the White House?

13. What future president was the Republican National Committee (RNC) chairman who formally requested President Nixon's resignation?

14. Name a write-in candidate who received one electoral vote and later became president.

15. Name three presidents who all occupied the office of president during the same year.

16. How many men defeated incumbent presidents to be elected to the highest office in the land?

17. In which room of the White House did First Lady Abigail Adams hang her laundry to dry?

18. What secret society did both President Bushes belong to while students at Yale University?

19. Whose inaugural address was the shortest in history?

20. Which president went around turning off lights that were not in use at the White House?

21. Who appointed future president George H. W. Bush to the position of head of the CIA?

22. Which state is the birthplace of seven presidents?

23. Who pays for the official White House portraits of the presidents and First Ladies?

24. How many letters did Abraham Lincoln receive daily while in office?

25. What did FDR and George H. W. Bush have in common?

26. Which president and First Lady loved to look at the stars and planets through their telescope on the roof of the White House?

27. When did former president Nixon choose not to use his Secret Service protection any longer?

28. Who did FDR insist must be in attendance at his final inauguration?

29. What was the last official function that JFK attended in the White House?

30. What is the significance of October 13, 2092?

Exclusive Chief Executive Power Is Yours

If You Answer This Question . . .

★ On George Washington's official portrait that hangs in the East Room of the White House, there was an error on the part of the artist. What is the error?

Answers to Noah's Ultimate Political Quiz

Governor Level

1. Leslie King (who later changed his name to Gerald Ford).

2. You must be 35 years old.

3. William Howard Taft (at Griffith Stadium in Washington, D.C., in 1910).

4. Franklin D. Roosevelt.

5. Ronald Reagan.

6. Beef, milk, dust, mold spores, weed and grass pollens, and cat dander.

7. Ronald Reagan.

8. Lyndon Johnson.

9. Thomas Jefferson, Abraham Lincoln, and Andrew Johnson.

10. Richard M. Nixon.

11. Republican.

12. George Washington, John Adams, and Thomas Jefferson.

13. John Adams.

14. James Monroe.

15. Thirty-two years old.

16. William Henry Harrison, John Tyler, Zachary Taylor, and Millard Fillmore.

17. William Howard Taft.

18. Thirty-five.

19. Abe Lincoln. (Six feet four inches tall.)

20. William Howard Taft.

21. James Madison.

22. Ronald Reagan.

23. Dwight Eisenhower.

24. Jimmy Carter.

25. Teddy Roosevelt. (John F. Kennedy was the youngest elected president.)

26. Ronald Reagan.

27. Gerald Ford.

28. Eight. (William Henry Harrison, Zachary Taylor, Abraham Lincoln, James Garfield, William McKinley, Warren Harding, Franklin D. Roosevelt, and John F. Kennedy.)

29. Abraham Lincoln, James Garfield, William McKinley, and John F. Kennedy.

30. Andrew Jackson, Harry S. Truman, Gerald Ford, and Ronald Reagan. (Teddy Roosevelt survived an assassination attempt after leaving office.)

U.S. House of Representatives Level

1. Andrew Johnson.

2. Abraham Lincoln.

3. Thomas Jefferson.

4. Rosewood.

5. Franklin D. Roosevelt.

6. George Washington—quarter, Thomas Jefferson—nickel, Abraham Lincoln—penny, Franklin D. Roosevelt—dime, Dwight Eisenhower—dollar, and John F. Kennedy—half-dollar.

7. Martin Van Buren.

8. Thomas Jefferson.

9. The $20 bill.

10. Ulysses S. Grant. (He was being treated for throat cancer.)

11. John Adams and Thomas Jefferson.

12. 140.

13. Gerald Ford, Jimmy Carter, George H. W. Bush, Bill Clinton, and George W. Bush—they are still living.

14. Harry S. Truman.

15. Dwight Eisenhower.

16. The twenty-second—it limited presidents to two full terms in office.

17. William McKinley.

18. Virginia.

19. The twenty-second and twenty-fourth president are the same man, Grover Cleveland. He served two nonconsecutive terms.

20. Lucy Webb Hayes.

21. Andrew Jackson (lost to John Quincy Adams), Samuel Tilden (lost to Rutherford B. Hayes), Grover Cleveland (lost to Benjamin Harrison), and Al Gore (lost to George W. Bush).

22. Speaker of the House.

23. John Adams, Herbert Hoover, Gerald Ford, and Ronald Reagan.

24. George Washington, Thomas Jefferson, Abraham Lincoln, Andrew Jackson, Ulysses S. Grant, William McKinley, Grover Cleveland, James Madison, and Woodrow Wilson.

25. William Henry Harrison and Zachary Taylor.

26. James Monroe.

27. Calvin Coolidge.

28. John Tyler.

29. He had smallpox.

30. Bill and Hillary Clinton.

U.S. Senator Level

1. James Monroe. (Monrovia, capital of Liberia in Africa.)

2. Thirty.

3. Six. (Andrew Jackson, Zachary Taylor, Millard Fillmore, James Buchanan, Abraham Lincoln, and James Garfield.)

4. George Washington (both terms) and James Monroe (second term).

5. $400,000.

6. Nelson Rockefeller.

7. Theodore Roosevelt.

8. Harry S. Truman.

9. Richard Nixon. In 1969 the Nixons had a one-lane alley built because they were both avid bowlers.

10. Ten years.

11. Harry S. Truman.

12. Harry S. Truman.

13. a. *It Can Be Done.*

14. He converted the indoor pool to a pressroom.

15. Thomas Jefferson.

16. Rutherford B. Hayes.

17. George W. Bush.

18. 18.07 acres.

19. In 1902, during Teddy Roosevelt's administration. In 1909 William Howard Taft expanded the West Wing.

20. Theodore Roosevelt.

21. He appointed a chief justice the night before Jefferson took the oath of office.

22. The East Room. (79 feet long, 37 feet wide.)

23. On the grounds of the U.S. Naval Observatory.

24. LBJ.

25. George W. Bush.

26. Hillary Clinton.

27. JFK—*Profiles in Courage.*

28. Harry S. Truman.

29. Thomas Jefferson.

30. Lou Hoover.

Vice President Level

1. James Garfield, Herbert Hoover, Harry S. Truman, Gerald Ford, George H. W. Bush, and Bill Clinton.

2. Vice president, Speaker of the House, president pro tempore of the Senate, secretary of state, secretary of the treasury.

3. 1.2 miles.

4. Thirty-five.

5. Herbert Hoover. (Hooveria.)

6. James Hoban.

7. George W. Bush.

8. Andrew Jackson.

9. Franklin D. Roosevelt. (In 1943.)

10. Gerald Ford.

11. Harry S. Truman and Richard Nixon.

12. Franklin Roosevelt. (Frances Perkins—secretary of labor.)

13. Six. (Madison, Monroe, Polk, Buchanan, Garfield, and Carter.)

14. 9B.

15. Yes, but it was not the future president Jimmy Carter, it was a chef named Jimmy Carter.

16. 12:00 noon on January 20.

17. The Oval Office.

18. Fala, Franklin D. Roosevelt's beloved dog.

19. William McKinley; it was his offering for church.

20. John F. Kennedy.

21. He was being treated with radioactive iodine for Graves' disease.

22. His mom.

23. George H. W. Bush.

24. Ronald Reagan.

25. John Adams, Thomas Jefferson, Martin Van Buren, and George H. W. Bush.

26. The leaders of the Building and Construction Trades Department of the AFL-CIO.

27. Ulysses S. Grant.

28. John Adams and Thomas Jefferson.

29. To shorten the outgoing president's lame-duck period.

30. Ronald Reagan.

"Hail to the Chief" Level

1. George McGovern.

2. John Quincy Adams.

3. Jimmy Carter.

4. John Adams and John Quincy Adams.

5. Calvin Coolidge.

6. H. Upmann Petit Coronas.

7. The president and the vice president.

8. Jacqueline Kennedy.

9. JFK received 49.7 percent and Richard Nixon received 49.6 percent.

10. John F. Kennedy and Richard Nixon.

11. Ronald Reagan. (He was president of the Screen Actors Guild.)

12. Harry S. Truman.

13. George H. W. Bush.

14. Ronald Reagan.

15. Martin Van Buren, William Henry Harrison, and John Tyler. (1841.)

16. Eight. (Andrew Jackson, William Henry Harrison, Benjamin Harrison, Woodrow Wilson, Franklin D. Roosevelt, Jimmy Carter, Ronald Reagan, and Bill Clinton.)

17. The East Room.

18. Skull and Bones.

19. George Washington's second inaugural address—135 words.

20. Lyndon Johnson.

21. Gerald Ford.

22. Ohio.

23. The White House Historical Association. (Through sales of books, prints, and artwork.)

24. Up to three hundred.

25. They both hated broccoli.

26. Jimmy and Rosalynn Carter.

27. Eleven years after leaving the White House.

28. All of his grandchildren.

29. An evening judiciary reception.

30. This is the year that George and Barbara Bush's time capsule will be opened. It contains a copy of *Millie's Book* by Barbara Bush and a letter from President George H. W. Bush.

Exclusive Chief Executive Power Is Yours

If You Answer This Question . . .

★ The title on one of the books under the table reads *"United Sates."*

Acknowledgments

Special Thanks to:

My Lord and Savior, for everything. I want to honor you in all I do!

My mom, for helping me research trivia and for all the typing. I love you!

My dad, for all of his love and support. I love you!

My special friend, JoLisa Hoover, who read my manuscript and encouraged me!

Mrs. Rougeau, my second-grade teacher, who was always willing to "talk presidents"!

My aunt Barbara, for my Web site and business cards to begin my campaigning early!

Mrs. Krig, my school librarian, who allowed me into the nonfiction section in first grade!

My editor, Jonathan Jao, for always seeking my opinion . . . and for being cool!

Random House, for such a great opportunity!

The Random House team that worked on this book and made it great!

All the folks at Progress for America. We are a good team!

Mr. Daniel Herns, my future attorney general, for all your wise counsel!

All of my friends and family, for loving me and promising to vote for me in 2032!

My church and school, Second Baptist, for teaching and encouraging me!

My fifth-grade teacher, Ms. Andersson, for reading and helping me edit my manuscript!

The FDR Presidential Library—Virginia Lewick, archivist— for all the good information!

The Gerald Ford Presidential Library, for answering my e-mails!

The George Bush Presidential Library, for allowing me to visit twenty-seven times and meet the forty-first leader of the free world, President George H. W. Bush!

Our nation's forty-two men who have served in the office of president and inspired me!

Bibliography

Books

Anthony, Carl Sferrazza. *America's First Families*. New York: Touchstone, 2000.

Buller, Jon, Susan Schade, Maryann Cocca-Leffler, Dana Regan, and Jill Weber. *Smart About the Presidents*. New York: Grosset & Dunlap, 2004.

Buller, Jon, Susan Schade, Dana Regan, Sally Warner, and Jill Weber. *Smart About the First Ladies*. New York: Grosset & Dunlap, 2005.

Couch, Ernie, comp. *Presidential Trivia*. Nashville: Rutledge Hill, 1966.

Davis, Kenneth C. *Don't Know Much About the Presidents*. New York: HarperCollins, 2002.

DeGregorio, William A. *The Complete Book of U.S. Presidents*. New York: Barnes & Noble, 2004.

Bibliography

Fuqua, Nell. *First Pets: Presidential Best Friends.* New York: Scholastic, 2004.

———. *U.S. Presidents: Feats & Foul-Ups: The Good, the Bad, and the Silly.* New York: Lemon Drop/Scholastic, 2003.

Kraft, Betsy Harvey. *Theodore Roosevelt: Champion of the American Spirit.* New York: Clarion Books, 2003.

Krull, Katherine. *Lives of the Presidents.* San Diego: Harcourt Brace, 1998.

Lang, J. Stephen. *The Complete Book of Presidential Trivia.* Gretna, LA: Pelican, 2001.

Matuz, Roger. *The Presidents Fact Book.* New York: Black Dog & Leventhal, 2004.

O'Brien, Cormac. *Secret Lives of the U.S. Presidents.* Philadelphia: Quirk, 2004.

Phillips, Louis. *Ask Me Anything About the Presidents.* New York: Avon, 1994.

Pitch, Anthony S. *Exclusively Presidential Trivia.* Potomac, MD: Mino, 2001.

———. *Exclusively White House Trivia.* Potomac, MD: Mino, 2002.

Seuling, Barbara. *The Last Cow on the White House Lawn.* New York: Scholastic, 1978.

Truman, Margaret. *The President's House: 1800 to the Present.* New York: Ballantine, 2003.

Valdez, David, comp. *George Herbert Walker Bush: A Photographic Profile.* College Station, TX: Texas A&M University Press, 1997.

Online Sources

Bumiller, Elisabeth. "White House Letter: President Bush's iPod." *The New York Times* on the Web, April 11, 2005. http://www.nytimes.com/2005/04/11/politics/11letter.html

http://www.classroomhelp.com/lessons/presidents

http://www.narsil.org (for Hoover, Carter, and Franklin Roosevelt information)

http://www.potus.com

http://www.whitehousehistory.org—the White House Historical Association

Personal Visits/Tours/Research

The George Bush Presidential Library and Museum

The Carter Center

The William J. Clinton Presidential Library and Museum

The Herbert Hoover Presidential Library and Museum

The Lyndon Baines Johnson Library and Museum

The John F. Kennedy Library and Museum

The Richard Nixon Library and Birthplace

The Ronald Reagan Presidential Library

Written Correspondence Sources

The Gerald R. Ford Presidential Library and Museum

The Franklin D. Roosevelt Presidential Library and Museum

DVD Series

The Presidents: The Lives and Legacies of the 43 Leaders of the United States. The History Channel/A&E Home Video, 2005.

About the Author

NOAH MCCULLOUGH is a ten-year-old fifth grader committed to preparing himself to be a U.S. president. His dream is to be the Republican Party nominee in 2032 and ultimately to be elected president. He has been interested in the political process since the famed 2000 election. As a kindergartner he had big questions about the electoral college, nominations, and platforms. Being an avid reader has helped him quench his thirst for knowledge of history and the men and women who have made it happen.

Noah has appeared on *The Tonight Show with Jay Leno* numerous times as a political whiz kid and correspondent. His wit and knowledge of U.S. history have been a hit with viewers. Noah was a Scholastic Kids Press Corps election reporter. He interviewed John Kerry and covered many election-related events as well as Inauguration 2005.

Inspired by the forty-two men who have led this country, Noah is motivated to be a leader when he grows up, but not just any leader . . . a great one. He continues his quest with an altruistic spirit, knowing that serving and loving others is the key to world peace and true happiness. Each year Noah helps to raise money for the Juvenile Diabetes Research Foundation. He is committed to helping raise money to fund research for a cure to this and other diseases that plague young people. Two of his cousins have type 1 diabetes, which makes Noah even more committed.

Noah's gift for speaking keeps him busy with engagements throughout the year. He is also a talented writer who feels blessed to be a newly published author. He is eager to begin work on his next project as soon as possible. Noah is driven in his pursuit to get more young people interested in history, politics, and their government. Besides history, he enjoys golf, basketball, and video games. People often ask him if he is going to run out of energy, because usually former presidents are writing, speaking, and playing golf. His reply is always, "I'm just getting started!" His mantra remains "Vote for me in 2032 on the Republican ticket!"